16-19 MATHEMATICS

Networks

Student text and unit guide

The School Mathematics Project

CAMBRIDGE
UNIVERSITY PRESS

Main authors	Chris Belsom
	Stan Dolan
	Sandra Haigh
	Ron Haydock
	Alan Knighton
	Paul Roder
	Thelma Wilson
Project Director	Stan Dolan

Initial work on this unit was carried out by Simon French, Sandra Haigh, Allan Humphreys and Les Proll at Leeds University.

The authors would like to give special thanks to Ann White for her help in preparing this book for publication.

Cartoons by Gordon Hendry

Drawings by Keyword

The authors and publishers would like to thank the following for supplying photographs:
cover – Henryk T. Kaiser/The Picture Cube
page 62 – Adam Hart-Davis/Science Photo Library

The authors and publishers would like to thank George Philip Ltd. for permission to reproduce the map (© 1976 George Philip) on page 78.

Published by the Press Syndicate of the University of Cambridge
The Pitt Building, Trumpington Street, Cambridge CB2 1RP
40 West 20th Street, New York, NY 10011-4211, USA
10 Stamford Road, Oakleigh, Victoria 3166, Australia

© Cambridge University Press 1994

First published 1994

Produced by 16–19 Mathematics, Southampton

· Printed in Great Britain by Scotprint Ltd., Musselburgh.

ISBN 0 521 46788 8

Contents and resources

Introduction to the unit

This unit has been designed so that it can be started early in an advanced level course. It is independent of other *16–19 Mathematics* texts and requires no mathematical prerequisites beyond GCSE.

The unit has been written to facilitate 'supported self-study'. In particular, all solutions and commentaries are in this text.

Chapter 1

Scheduling problems concerned with ensuring the best use of time and resources are used to introduce the concept of a network. In this chapter, students meet the first algorithm of the unit – the process of making a forward and a reverse pass to determine a critical path.

In practice, much more elementary techniques are used as well as critical path analysis and the chapter also includes a consideration of key event plans, Gantt charts and resource levelling. Students are encouraged to employ the methods of this chapter on a project of their own choosing. This will help improve their appreciation of the relationship between mathematical techniques and the practicalities of real situations.

Chapter 2

Having met a practical use of graphs in Chapter 1, students are now introduced to some general graph theoretical ideas which will be of use in later chapters.

Traversability, circuits and trees are developed from historical examples and, in particular, through their applications in electrical circuit theory and organic chemistry. Other ideas which are important for later work are also met, including directed graphs, weighted graphs and incidence tables.

The chapter ends with a consideration of planarity. This has practical relevance, for example, in the production of printed circuit boards and also has considerable mathematical importance in the relationship between a purely geometrical concept and arithmetical considerations such as Euler's formula.

Chapter 3

This chapter contains various examples of problems which involve making connections so as to minimise a quantity such as length or cost. Two methods of solving this type of problem are given, Prim's algorithm and Kruskal's algorithm. Both these algorithms are based upon the important idea of 'greediness' – choosing the 'best' edge at each stage. Although greediness works for this type of problem it is important for students to appreciate that it **may** not work for all types of problem. Whilst beyond this scope of this course, there is a need for both:

- a rigorous, precise statement of any algorithmic procedure;
- a proof of the correctness of the algorithm.

Chapter 4

The type of problem studied in this chapter is similar to that of Chapter 3 but here the concern is to find the best connection between just two points (rather than between all the points).

Students will discover that for this problem the type of greedy algorithm employed in the previous chapter does not always yield the required solution. Two different methods, Dijkstra's algorithm and dynamic programming, are considered and compared.

Chapter 5

This chapter is concerned with the two problems of:

- finding a shortest route along all the edges of a graph;
- finding a shortest route visiting all the vertices.

The first of these can be solved easily using the ideas of traversability covered in Chapter 2. Although the second problem sounds similar it has proved to be very difficult to solve in terms of computational complexity. Consequently, various heuristic methods are often employed. These produce good but not necessarily optimal solutions.

Miscellaneous exercise

The unit ends with an extended exercise, covering a range of problems. This should emphasise the need for students to learn to recognise problem types and select appropriate methods of solution.

1 Critical path analysis

1.1 Scheduling activities

Projects as varied as building a motorway link, launching a new chocolate bar onto the market and designing a new mathematics curriculum all involve careful planning. In each case it is important to schedule a large number of interrelated activities in such a way that no individual activity is **unnecessarily** held up because of a failure to complete another activitity.

To ensure the best use of manpower and resources, mathematical techniques are now widely used in industry. Many of these techniques were developed by the US Navy, in particular for its Polaris missile project. The methods depend upon first drawing a **network** of the activities.

Shown below is part of a diagram used by Sainsbury in their production process. This refers to advertising and represents only a small part of the complete process.

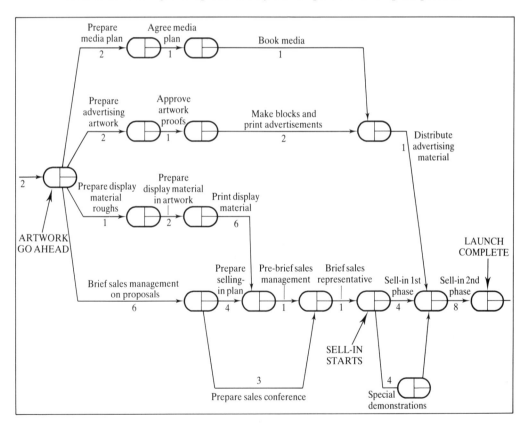

When you break down a task into its individual activities you must choose how finely you wish to subdivide the task. In practice, senior managers are likely to split projects into fairly broad activities which are then subdivided into a more detailed plan at operational levels within an organisation.

1

The procedure of producing an overall plan can be illustrated by converting a recipe into a network diagram.

GRANDMA'S SPONGE SANDWICH

110 g self-raising flour   1 teaspoon baking powder
 75 g margarine or butter   1 tablespoon milk
110 g caster sugar $\frac{1}{2}$ tablespoon water
  2   large eggs   jam for filling

Preheat oven to 190°C, gas regulo 5. Cream the fat and sugar. Add milk, water and eggs, beating well. Fold flour into mixture. Put in greased tins and bake for 10 minutes. Allow to cool and fill with jam or other filling.

An appropriate list of activities for the sponge sandwich might include such items as the following.

Activity	Duration (minutes)	Preceding activities
Weigh the flour	$\frac{1}{4}$	–
Fold flour into mixture	$\frac{1}{2}$	Mixing in the eggs and liquid. Weighing the flour.
...	...	...

These activities can then be drawn as a network so that each activity is to the right of all the activities which must be completed before it can be started. The times in minutes are also shown in the network.

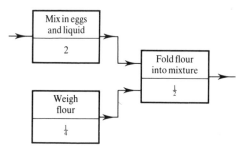

(a) Subdivide the task of making the sponge sandwich into a set of activities.

(b) Decide on suitable times for each activity.

(c) Draw a network for the task and hence estimate the least time required to make a sponge sandwich.

(d) How many people are needed if the sponge is to be made in the least possible time?

1.2   Start times

One purpose of careful scheduling is to minimise the time spent waiting for activities to be completed. Suppose, for example, that a Parents' Association plans to improve the garden area near the school entrance. A working party is gathered together and the tasks to be performed are as shown in the table.

Activity	Preceding activity	Time (hours)
A Clear and prepare site		1
B Set edging	A	1
C Lay hardcore for path·	B	$\frac{1}{2}$
D Spread gravel on path	C	$\frac{1}{2}$
E Dig and fertilise ground	A	2
F Plant shrubs	C, E	1
G Tidy site	D, F	$\frac{1}{2}$

The total time (of $6\frac{1}{2}$ hours) can be considerably reduced by working on some of the tasks simultaneously. A simple network diagram might be as shown.

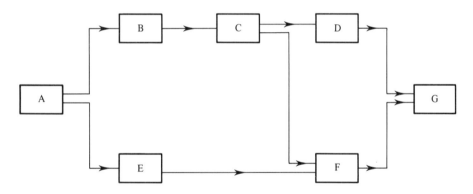

Suppose that the activities in the above network can start at 9 a.m.

(a)   What is the earliest possible time for completing the work?

(b)   To achieve this earliest possible completion time, what is:

   (i)   the earliest possible start time for each activity;

   (ii)   the latest possible finishing time for each activity?

For complex networks it can be helpful to write earliest possible start times and latest possible finish times on the network. For example, as follows:

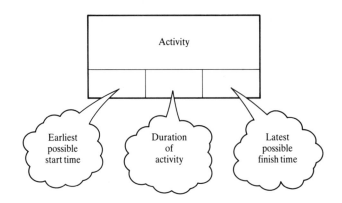

In practice, computers are used to draw the networks. They are also used to calculate start and finish times using a simple procedure.

All activities which have no preceding activities are given a start time of zero. Working through the network from left to right, the earliest start time of each activity is found by considering the activities which must precede it.

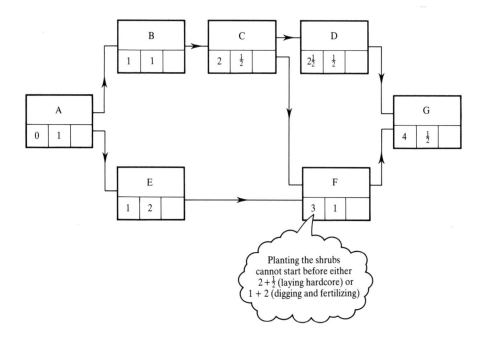

The process of calculating earliest possible start times by working from left to right through a network is called a **forward pass**.

- When all earliest start times have been found, latest finishing times can be found by working back through the network from right to left. When an activity immediately precedes several activities then the least value of

latest finish time – duration

must be chosen.

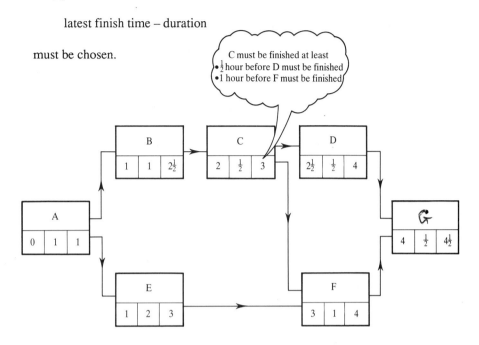

C must be finished at least
• $\frac{1}{2}$ hour before D must be finished
• 1 hour before F must be finished

The process of working from right to left, calculating finish times, is called a **reverse pass**.

You will notice that for four of the activities

earliest possible start time + duration = latest possible finish time

For example,

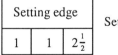

Plant shrubs		
3	1	4

has $3 + 1 = 4$.

Such activities are called **critical activities.** It is essential to complete all critical activities on time if the whole project is to be finished in the least possible time.

The **float** of a non-critical activity is the amount by which the latest finish time is greater than its earliest start time plus duration.

Setting edge		
1	1	$2\frac{1}{2}$

Setting the edging has a float of $2\frac{1}{2} - (1 + 1) = \frac{1}{2}$ hour.

The existence of float means an activity can start later than its earliest possible start time and/or you can take longer to complete the activity.

Any network will have a least one **critical path** – a path from left to right through the
network consisting only of critical activities. For example:

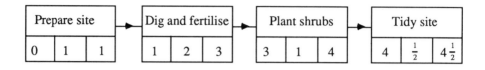

Prepare site			Dig and fertilise			Plant shrubs			Tidy site		
0	1	1	1	2	3	3	1	4	4	$\frac{1}{2}$	$4\frac{1}{2}$

Exercise 1

1   The schedule for a small construction project is as shown. All durations are in
days.

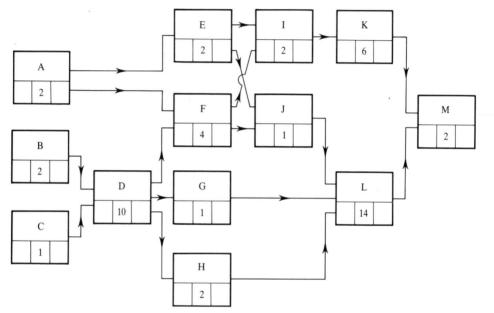

(a)   Find all earliest possible start times and latest possible finishing times.

(b)   Hence find a critical path.

(c)   Which activity has the greatest float?

2   Various problems may occur when carrying out a project. Investigate the effect
on the construction project of question 1 if:

(a)   activity F requires 6 days;

(b)   activity G requires 6 days;

(c)   activity I requires 6 days.

In each case, find out whether the critical path changes.

3 In practice, it may not be necessary for one activity to finish completely before another can start. Decide how you could display the following situations in a network diagram.

(a) Paint takes 8 hours to dry but wallpapering can start midway through this period.

(b) Laying carpets can only occur 24 hours after the paintwork is dry.

4 A company specialising in organising and catering for special functions uses the plan outlined below to prepare for a celebration dance with a rock band, when the full team of staff is available. The estimated times for each activity are shown in hours.

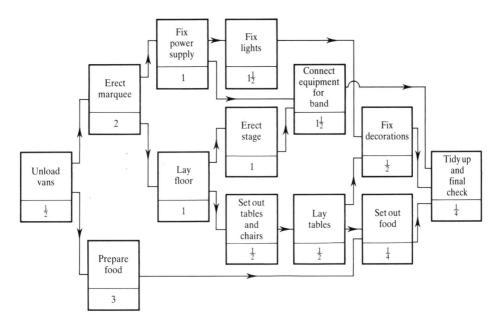

(a) Find all earliest possible start times, latest possible finishing times and identify a critical path.

(b) To ensure that all preparations are complete by 6.30 p.m. what is the latest time at which the vans must arrive on site?

(c) If only one electrician is available then the arrangements for the band must be made after the lights have been fixed up. What effect will this have on the total time required for the preparations? Will there be any change to the critical path?

(d) For a similar event where the band do not require any special equipment to be installed, how much time will be saved compared with the standard plan? Identify the critical activities in this case.

1.3 Resource levelling

Networks are widely used for planning complex projects with long timescales. In practice, computers are used to convert information about the activities into a network diagram. A computer program is also likely to be used to print out timings of various activities which will ensure that other tasks are not held up. Using a computer enables the planner to see rapidly the effect of modifying the plan in various ways. In particular, it is easy to update the plan in the light of changing circumstances.

According to the British Standards Institution guidelines, a computer application should be used if the number of activities is greater than 100 and updating occurs more than once a month (BS 6046, Part 3, 1981).

Some major disadvantages of using networks are that:

- they are not understood by most people;

- they do not show the resources needed. ('Resources' include the people available to do the work.)

In consequence they tend to be used only on highly complex and long-term projects. Some other, simpler techniques, are therefore in common use.

One of the simplest forms of plan consists of a list of **key events** and the time each event is planned to occur. The following might be an appropriate form of plan drawn up by a subject officer at an examinations board.

MATHEMATICS PAPERS	
Date	Key events
March 1	Draft examination papers circulated amongst examiners for comment.
April 6	Meeting of examiners to prepare examination papers for typesetting.
May 10	Printed papers circulated to members of preparatory sub-committee.
September 24	Meeting of sub-committee to approve papers.
October 20	Modified proofs of papers sent to printers.
November 5	Final proofs of examination papers checked and returned to printers.

> **Draw up a key events plan for the catering team considered in question 4(b) of Exercise 1.**

Perhaps the most widely used method of scheduling events is to show activities as bars against a timescale. Such bar charts are often called **Gantt charts** after the person credited with developing this planning technique.

Suppose a network diagram for the start of a building project is as shown:

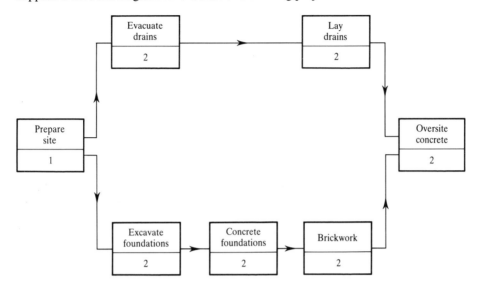

Then an equivalent Gantt chart might be as follows:

Activity	Dates: July									
	Th 7	F 8	Sa 9	Su 10	M 11	Tu 12	W 13	Th 14	F 15	Sa 16
A Prepare site	■									
B Excavate drains		■	■							
C Lay drains					■	■				
D Excavate foundations		■	■							
E Concrete foundations					■	■				
F Brickwork to ground floor level							■	■		
G Lay oversite concrete									■	■

A Gantt chart is a visual representation of a plan which most people find easy to understand. It is also easy to see from a Gantt chart what resources will be needed at what times. This important feature of any plan will be considered next.

So far, you have considered only the scheduling of activities to a timescale. In practice, the duration of any activity may depend upon the resources used, these resources being limited by the total budget. In an extreme case, missing an agreed deadline might incur such high costs (because of penalty clauses in a contract) that it may be sensible to put in extra resources at an apparently uneconomic level to work at some critical activity.

It is usually more important for the planner to arrange the schedule so that a resource such as skilled manpower is used as evenly as possible throughout the project. In general, you are more likely to obtain good quality labour at a reasonable price if you require 1 person for 30 days rather than 30 people for 1 day. A few of the options a planner has are:

• to reduce the allocation of resources to a non-critical activity;

• to alter the start times of non-critical activities;

• to change the plan by allocating resources in a different way.

Suppose that each of the activities shown on the Gantt chart require six labourers.

A resources diagram for the labour required would then be as shown.

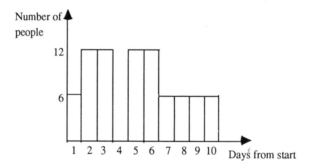

> **Suggest a way of levelling the labour requirement for this project.**

   TASKSHEET 1 – *Manufacturing barbecues*

10

Exercise 2

1 A piece of derelict land is to be turned into a garden, which will include a pond with a wildlife area round it, a shrubbery with a path through it, a rockery and a paved area. The activity table below is drawn up for the work.

	Activity	Preceding activities	Number of person-days
A	Prepare and fence site		4
B	Dig pond	A	1
C	Fill pond and put plants around edges	B	1
D	Plant and seed wildlife area	C	2
E	Lay path	A	2
F	Plant shrubbery	E	1
G	Lay paved area	A	2
H	Build rockery	A	1
I	Plant rockery and tubs for paved area	G, H	1
J	Check and tidy whole area	all	1

Each activity is to be completed by one person, except for A, where two people may work together.

(a) Draw up a network diagram for the whole process of making the garden, assuming:

   (i) there are no limitations on the labour available, but using the labour as efficiently as possible:

   (ii) that only two people are available to do the work.

(b) Draw Gantt charts and resources graphs corresponding to your networks for parts (i) and (ii) above.

2 A group of writers is planning to produce a mathematical textbook consisting of five chapters. At an initial meeting it is agreed that the times needed to write first versions of the chapters are:

   Chapter 1 – 4 weeks, Chapter 2 – 6 weeks, Chapter 3 – 6 weeks,
   Chapter 4 – 7 weeks, Chapter 5 – 4 weeks

After the meeting, each writer will go away and work on one or two chapters. When all the first versions (or drafts) are completed, they will be circulated, so that all the writers read all of the chapters. This process will take 3 weeks, at the end of which there will be a second meeting. After this meeting the final versions of the chapters will be written. They decide that this should take:

   Chapter 1 – 3 weeks, Chapter 2 – 2 weeks, Chapter 3 – 4 weeks,
   Chapter 4 – 3 weeks, Chapter 5 – 4 weeks

(It is not necessary for the person who produced the first version of a chapter to produce the final version of the same chapter.)

When the second versions are completed, they are sent to the editor, who takes 5 weeks to check the solutions to the exercises and prepare the manuscript for the publisher.

(a) Complete the activity table below for the whole process.

Activity		Preceding activities	Number of weeks
A	Hold the first meeting		4
B	Draft Chapter 1	A	4
C	Draft Chapter 2	A	~~4~~ 6
⋮	⋮	⋮	⋮
G	Circulate material and have second meeting	A, B, C, D, E, F	3
⋮		⋮	⋮

(b) Draw Gantt charts for the whole process:

    (i) assuming that four writers work on the book throughout;

    (ii) if one of the four writers has to go abroad after the second meeting, so can only help with the first version of a chapter or chapters.

(c) For the process of (b) part (ii), calculate the latest possible date on which the first meeting must be held if the manuscript has to be ready for the publisher on 30 June.

(d) Draw resource diagrams for the period of writing the second versions for situations (i) and (ii).

Projects

Choose a project for which you must prepare a plan. Some possibilities include:

- producing the first issue of a school magazine;
- organising a fund raising activity;
- planning a family's move of house;
- resurfacing a stretch of motorway;
- building a house.

Whatever you choose, you should use a network to identify critical activities. Show that you have considered the availability of resources and the total cost.

Ideally, you should consider building some flexibility into your plan in case of unforeseen problems arising and you should have contingency plans available in case of possible problems that you have identified.

After working through this chapter you should:

1   know how to construct a precedence network diagram;

2   be able to use a forward pass through a network to determine the minimum completion time;

3   be able to use a reverse pass through a network to determine the critical activities;

4   know how to calculate the float for an activity;

5   be able to construct a Gantt chart;

6   be aware that relatively simple techniques such as key events planning and Gantt charts are commonly used;

7   appreciate that planning must involve considering the availability of resources and the total cost of the plan.

Manufacturing barbecues

Adam and Brian decide to set up a business manufacturing barbecues. They have broken the manufacturing process down into four stages which must be completed in the following order:

- cutting out the sheet metal (30 minutes);
- shaping and welding the barbecue (45 minutes);
- finishing and painting (60 minutes);
- bolting on the fittings and packaging the product (30 minutes).

They cannot both be working on the same barbecue at the same time.

They must wait at least 20 minutes for the metal to cool after welding before they can start finishing and painting. The paint takes 16 hours to dry.

They have to borrow money from the bank to set up the business and so they plan to buy just one machine for cutting sheet metal, one machine for shaping sheet metal, one welding torch, one spray gun for painting and a grinder for finishing.

Each barbecue requires $2\frac{3}{4}$ hours labour in its production and if they each work $8\frac{1}{4}$ hours a day they should be able to produce 6 barbecues per day.

1   Design a work schedule which enables them to do this and represent your solution on a Gantt chart.

2   When they look at the schedule they notice that the machines are only being used for part of the day. Should they employ an extra person to increasing efficiency?

2 Graphs

2.1 The Königsberg bridges

The father of graph theory was the Swiss mathematician Leonhard Euler (1707 – 1783). According to a well-known story, he heard of a problem which had intrigued the citizens of Königsberg in East Prussia since the beginning of the fifteenth century.

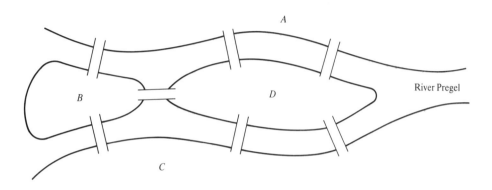

Königsberg lay near the mouth of the River Pregel, which divided the city into four parts (A, B, C and D), two of them being on the north and south banks of the river and two on islands. These four parts were connected by seven bridges. On Sunday afternoons people would stroll about the city idly pondering this problem:

> Could a walk take us over each of the seven bridges once
> only and return us to our starting point?

The genius of Euler lay in abstracting the essential connectedness of Königsberg in the simplest way. He represented the land masses by points (vertices) and the bridges by lines (edges).

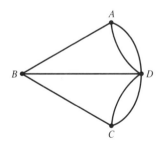

The result is a line drawing with seven edges and four vertices.

In 1736, Euler used this simple representation to prove that it was **not** possible to find a walk crossing each bridge precisely once. In fact, he generalised the problem and was able to determine precisely which arrangements of land masses and bridges could be traversed in the required way.

(a) **Show that the line drawing accurately represents the way in which land masses are connected by bridges.**

(b) **Count the number of edges at each vertex.**

(c) **Hence explain why the seven bridges walk is impossible.**

TASKSHEET 1 – *Traversability*

> In a line drawing, a trace which includes every edge just once is called (in honour of Euler):
>
> • an *eulerian trail* if it is closed (that is, finishes where it started);
>
> • a *semi-eulerian trail* if it is not closed.

A trace may be named by listing its vertices in order. For example,

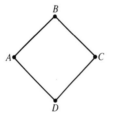

ABCDA is an eulerian trail.

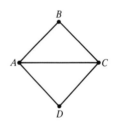

ABCADC is a semi-eulerian trail.

> **For each of the drawings below name an eulerian trail or a semi-eulerian trail, as appropriate.**

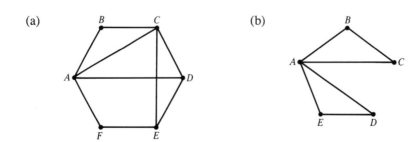

(a)

(b)

2.2　What is a graph?

The word 'graph' comes from the Greek *graphe*, meaning 'writing', but it has come to be used for extensions of writing as in 'phonograph' and 'polygraph' and for pictures as in 'photograph' and 'graphic artist'. In mathematics you will have used 'graph' in connection with statistical charts and cartesian plots.

In the sense to be used in this book, a graph is simply a line drawing showing the essential structure of a system. The critical path analysis (CPA) networks of Chapter 1 can all be represented by graphs, as can road and rail networks, molecular structures and electrical networks. For example:

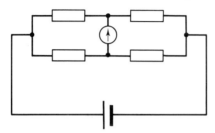 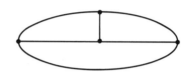

A Wheatstone bridge　　　　　　　　The underlying graph

In a graph, the points where **edges** meet or end are called **vertices**. The graph for the Wheatstone bridge has 6 edges and 4 vertices.

> **(a)　Redraw the CPA network given below as a graph of vertices and edges only.**
>
> **(b)　How many vertices are there?**
>
> **(c)　How many edges?**

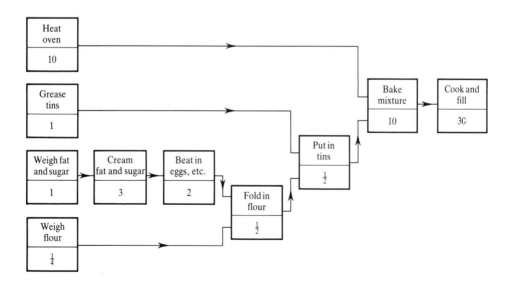

Three of the features of graphs which are especially important in applications of graph theory are **paths**, **circuits** and **spanning trees**.

A **path** is a sequence of vertices such that each pair of successive vertices is joined by an edge and no vertex is passed through more than once.

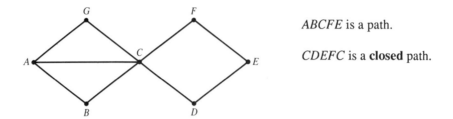

ABCFE is a path.

CDEFC is a **closed** path.

This idea has already been met in Chapter 1, where it was important to find critical paths through a network.

> **In the graph above, how many different paths are there from *A* to *E*?**

A **circuit** is a closed path i.e. one which starts and ends on the same vertex. In the graph above, *ACGA* and *CDEFC* are both circuits. The development of graph theory was given a considerable boost in 1847 when the German physicist Gustav Kirchoff (1824 – 1887) discovered how the currents in each branch of an electrical network could be determined by a system of linear equations. These equations were found by applying Kirchoff's laws to circuits of the underlying graph. However, even in a case as simple as that of the Wheatstone bridge, the underlying graph will have a large number of circuits.

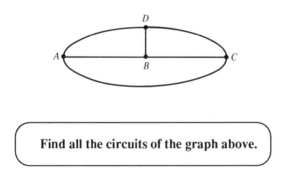

> **Find all the circuits of the graph above.**

Kirchoff was able to say precisely which circuits it was necessary to consider. Perhaps surprisingly, these depended only on the structure of the underlying graph and not on the particular electrical components such as cells, capacitors or resistors that were being considered.

Graphs without any circuits were also found to have important applications. In 1857, the English mathematician and lawyer Arthur Cayley (1821 – 1895) recognised the relevance of graph theory to the structure of molecules of the saturated hydrocarbons, three of which are shown below.

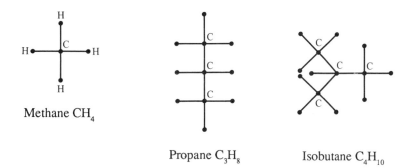

Methane CH_4

Propane C_3H_8 Isobutane C_4H_{10}

The graphs of the molecules have certain properties in common.

- They are **connected**. For any two points on the graph, a path can be found from one of the points to the other.

- They have no circuits.

- Each vertex corresponding to a carbon atom is at the junction of four edges whereas each vertex corresponding to a hydrogen atom is incident with only one edge. The number of edges meeting at a vertex is called the **order** of the vertex.

Connected graphs with no circuits are known as **trees**. Cayley studied saturated hydrocarbons with a given number of carbon atoms by considering trees in which each vertex had order 1 or 4.

If a connected graph has a circuit then any edge of that circuit can be deleted without disconnecting the graph. Deleting the edges in this way will result in a tree which connects all the vertices of the original graph. Such a tree is called a **spanning tree**. Deleting a different choice of edges may result in a completely different spanning tree.

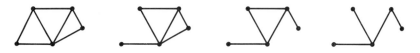

Successive stages in the formation of a spanning tree.

Spanning trees were extremely important in Kirchoff's work. For example, one of the possible spanning trees for the Wheatstone bridge is as shown.

19

The dotted lines show the three edges which have been deleted. Reinstating each one of these edges in turn yields three circuits.

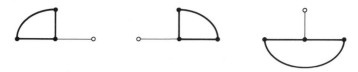

Kirchoff was able to prove that, from any chosen spanning tree, this construction **always** gave a minimal set of circuits to which his laws needed to be applied. This insight was of considerable value when dealing with complicated electrical networks.

Exercise 1

1   For a given graph, state conditions on the orders of the vertices if the graph is to be traversable with:

    (a)   an eulerian trail   (b)   a semi-eulerian trail

2   Draw all the trees which have:

    (a)   4 vertices   (b)   5 vertices

3   For the various trees you have met, draw up a table of the form

Number of vertices	Number of edges

What result appears to be true generally for any tree?

4   The underlying graph for a saturated hydrocarbon with n carbon atoms has n vertices of order 4. By considering the examples given in the text, conjecture how many vertices of order 1 (i.e. hydrogen atoms) such a graph will have.

5   (a)   Draw the underlying graph for this circuit which uses a light dependent resistor (LDR) to switch on a light when night falls.

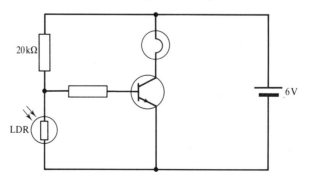

    (b)   How many different spanning trees does the underlying graph possess?

2.3　Incidence tables

The ways in which the vertices of a graph are connected can be shown using a table.

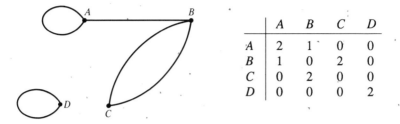

	A	B	C	D
A	2	1	0	0
B	1	0	2	0
C	0	2	0	0
D	0	0	0	2

Here a graph is shown with its **vertex–vertex incidence table**. Note how an edge connecting a vertex to itself (called a **loop**) is counted twice in the table.

> **(a)**　What is given by the sum of the entries in each row?
>
> **(b)**　Which other kinds of tables could be used to represent a graph?

When two graphs show the same connectedness they are said to be **isomorphic** and are regarded as being the same in graph theory. One way of demonstrating that two graphs are isomorphic is to show that their tables are 'the same'.

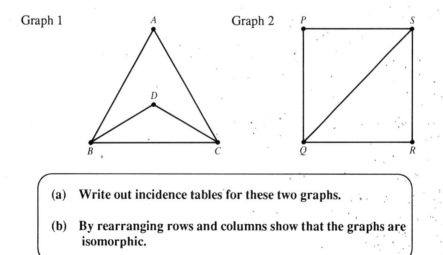

> **(a)**　Write out incidence tables for these two graphs.
>
> **(b)**　By rearranging rows and columns show that the graphs are isomorphic.

The isomorphism of two graphs is usually shown by writing out a correspondence between their vertices. The two graphs shown above are isomorphic under the correspondence

$$A \leftrightarrow P, \ B \leftrightarrow Q, \ C \leftrightarrow S, \ D \leftrightarrow R$$

In many graphs the edges are directed. For example, the underlying graph of the kind of network seen in Chapter 1 would normally be drawn with arrows on the edges, like this.

This is called a directed graph, abbreviated to **digraph**. From now on a distinction will be made between graphs (undirected) and digraphs.

Which of these might best be represented by a digraph?

  * A network of roads in a rural area.
  * A network of streets in a city centre.
  * A DC electrical network.
  * An AC electrical network.
  * A family tree.

Incidence tables may be used to represent digraphs.

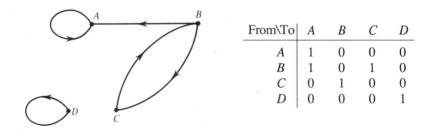

From\To	A	B	C	D
A	1	0	0	0
B	1	0	1	0
C	0	1	0	0
D	0	0	0	1

(a) What is given by the sum of the entries in each row?

(b) Why is this table not symmetrical about its main diagonal?

As with graphs, digraphs are isomorphic when they may be represented by the same table.

Exercise 2

1 Construct a vertex–vertex incidence table for the graph of the Königsberg bridges.

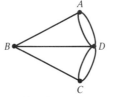

2 These three graphs are isomorphic. Show why, by appropriate labelling of vertices.

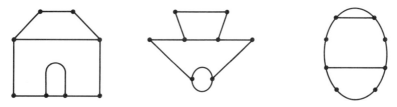

3 Find which two of the digraphs shown below are isomorphic. Demonstrate the isomorphism by labelling vertices appropriately.

(a)   (b)

(c)   (d)

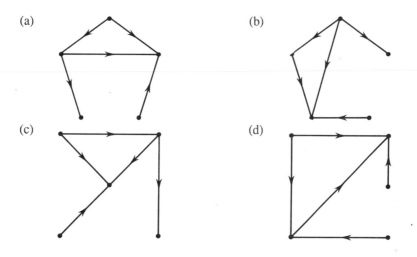

4E (a) Explain why there is only one structural form of propane.

(b) Show that there are two possible forms of butane C_4H_{10}.

(c) How many possible forms are there of C_5H_{12}?

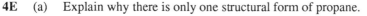

2.4 Graphs in practice

As you have seen, graphs consist of edges and vertices and a general definition says very little more.

> **A graph consists of a set of vertices and a set of edges. Each edge links two distinct vertices or links a single vertex to itself, forming a loop.**

Under this definition a graph might look like this.

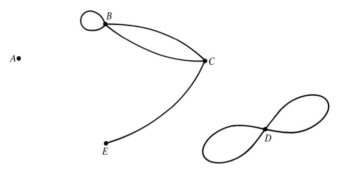

Here, *A* and *D* are disconnected vertices and *A* has no incident edges. The other vertices are connected: *E* is connected directly to *C* and indirectly to *B*; *B* and *C* are **multiply connected**, by two edges.

> **Write down the orders of the five vertices.**

Although such a graph must be included in the theory it is unlikely to be of much practical interest.

> **Think of several different networks of practical importance: air routes, oil pipe lines and so on. In each case decide what degree of connectedness is:**
>
> • **essential;**
> • **desirable;**
> • **undesirable.**

You probably decided that in practice loops, multiple connections and isolated vertices are usually undesirable. Generally it is essential that the vertices should be connected, directly or indirectly. Often, further connections are desirable.

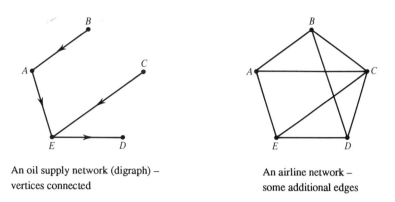

An oil supply network (digraph) –
vertices connected

An airline network –
some additional edges

In the airline network there are several circuits, such as (*ABCA*) allowing a round tour. The oil supply network has no circuits. As has been mentioned, such a connected graph with no circuits is called a tree.

The diagrams below illustrate other terms used in graph theory.

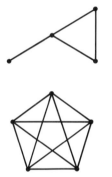

A **simple** graph contains no loops or multiple connections.

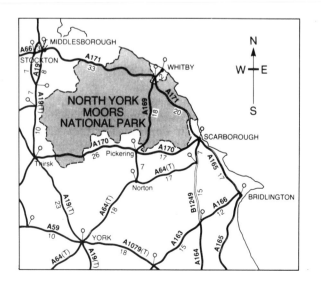

A **complete** graph is simple and every pair of vertices is joined by an edge. The complete graph on *n* vertices is called K_n. K_5 is illustrated.

On a road map, distances in miles or kilometres are often marked on the links (edges) between towns (vertices).

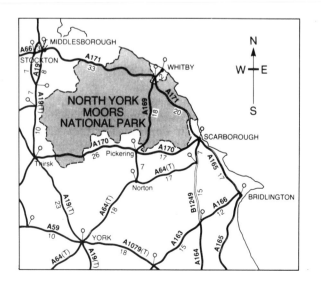

In later chapters you will be concerned with finding optimal routes through networks. This may mean simply finding the shortest possible distance for a journey. However, besides representing distances the numbers on edges may represent times, fuel consumption, cost and so on. A general term covering all these cases is the **weight** of an edge.

> A *weighted graph* is one in which a number is associated with each edge.

Exercise 3

1 (a)   (b)   (c)

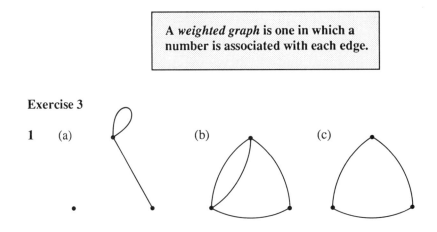

Complete the table.

	connected	simple	complete
(a)	x		
(b)	✓		
(c)			

What notation is used for graph (c)?

2 How many edges has:

(a) K_4 (b) K_n?

3

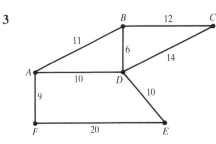

Draw up what you consider the most appropriate vertex–vertex table for this weighted graph.

26

2.5   Planar graphs

The silicon chips used in data processors contain printed circuits on flat platelets.

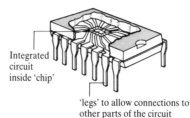

Integrated
circuit
inside 'chip'

'legs' to allow connections to
other parts of the circuit

In such a network it is essential that metal conductors should not cross. The graph formed by the terminals (vertices) and conductors (edges) is then said to be **plane.**

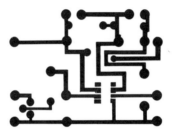

It may be that although a graph is not plane it can be made so by redirecting edges between certain vertices, maintaining the same connections (and not going into a third dimension).

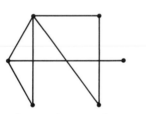

A non-plane graph.

Its plane equivalent.

Any graph which is plane or can be made plane in this way is said to be **planar.**

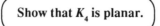

Show that K_4 is planar.

In the design of printed circuits, when the graph of a circuit is not planar a further platelet is needed. One of the more recent developments of graph theory is concerned with the 'thickness' of graphs, an abstract concept corresponding to the number of platelets that are needed.

In investigating graphs for planarity a useful tool is **Euler's formula**. Besides vertices and edges a plane graph contains well-defined **faces**, finite or infinite, bounded wholly or partly by the edges of the graph.

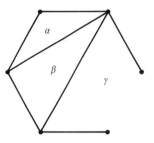

This plane graph has three faces, α, β, and γ. α and β are finite but γ is infinite. α and β are both wholly bounded by three edges, γ is partly bounded by six edges.

Euler discovered the following formula.

> **For a connected plane graph with v vertices, e edges and f faces,**
>
> $$v - e + f = 2$$

(a) Verify Euler's formula for the plane graph above.

(b) Draw K_4 as a plane graph and verify Euler's formula for this graph.

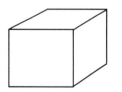

TASKSHEET 2 – K_5 is non-planar

Euler's formula for connected plane graphs also holds for 3-dimensional solids. Can you see why?

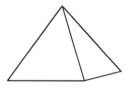

Cube: $v = 8$, $e = 12$, $f = 6$ Pyramid: $v = 5$, $e = 8$, $f = 5$

After working through this chapter you should:

1   understand the terms connected, simple, complete, plane, planar and weighted, as applied to graphs and digraphs;

2   understand the terms path, circuit and spanning tree;

3   be able to find the orders of the vertices of a graph and hence determine whether it contains an eulerian or semi-eulerian trail;

4   be able to draw up the incidence table of a graph and vice versa;

5   be able to demonstrate the isomorphism of graphs and digraphs;

6   be able to use Euler's formula for a connected plane graph;

7   appreciate the wide range of networks to which graph theory may be applied.

Traversability

1

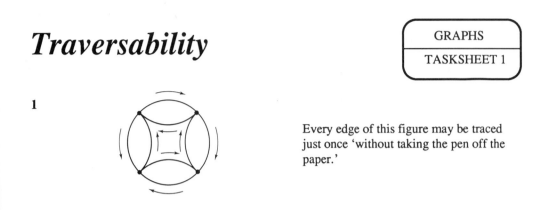

Every edge of this figure may be traced just once 'without taking the pen off the paper.'

Explain why this is possible starting from any one of its vertices.

In some cases a trace can be found which traverses every edge just once but the start point can not be freely chosen.

2

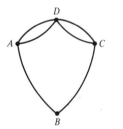

Show that for this drawing such a trace can start from vertex *A* but not from vertex *B*. How does the trace differ essentially from the one given in question 1?

3 For each of the drawings below decide which of the following is true:

(a) every edge can be traversed just once in a trace starting from any vertex;

(b) every edge can be traversed just once in a trace starting only from selected vertices;

(c) no trace exists.

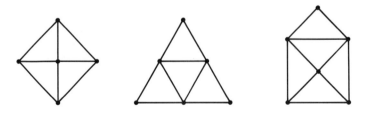

4 For each of the drawings of question 3, count the number of edges meeting at each vertex. Explain how such a count determines to which of the three categories of question 3 the drawing belongs.

Invent three drawings, one in each category, to illustrate your explanation.

To which category does the 'Königsberg bridge' drawing belong?

K_5 is non-planar

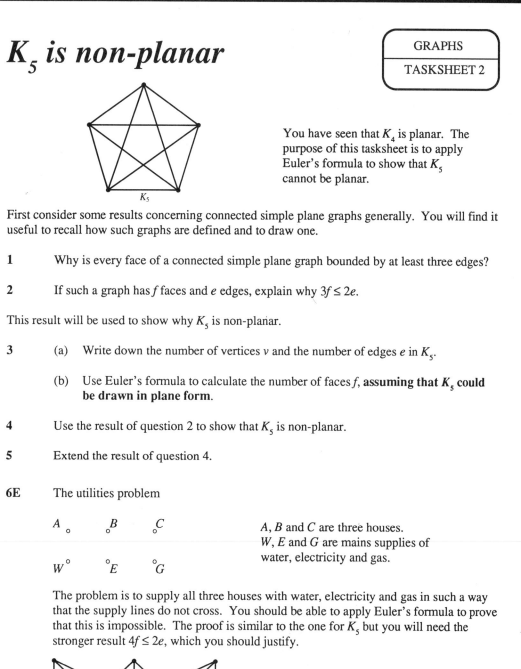

K_5

You have seen that K_4 is planar. The purpose of this tasksheet is to apply Euler's formula to show that K_5 cannot be planar.

First consider some results concerning connected simple plane graphs generally. You will find it useful to recall how such graphs are defined and to draw one.

1   Why is every face of a connected simple plane graph bounded by at least three edges?

2   If such a graph has f faces and e edges, explain why $3f \le 2e$.

This result will be used to show why K_5 is non-planar.

3   (a)   Write down the number of vertices v and the number of edges e in K_5.

   (b)   Use Euler's formula to calculate the number of faces f, **assuming that K_5 could be drawn in plane form**.

4   Use the result of question 2 to show that K_5 is non-planar.

5   Extend the result of question 4.

6E   The utilities problem

$A_{\circ}$ $_{\circ}B$ $_{\circ}C$

W° $^{\circ}E$ $^{\circ}G$

A, B and C are three houses.
W, E and G are mains supplies of water, electricity and gas.

The problem is to supply all three houses with water, electricity and gas in such a way that the supply lines do not cross. You should be able to apply Euler's formula to prove that this is impossible. The proof is similar to the one for K_5 but you will need the stronger result $4f \le 2e$, which you should justify.

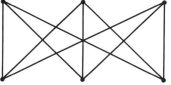

The 'utilities' graph is known formally as the **complete bipartite graph $K_{3,3}$**.

In 1930 the Polish mathematician Kuratowski proved that the only non-planar graphs were those 'containing' K_5 or $K_{3,3}$. To understand what he meant by 'containing' and see a proof of his theorem you could read, for example, Robin Wilson's *Introduction to Graph Theory* (Longman).

3 Spanning trees

3.1 Making connections

The diagram shows road links between five towns in the north of England, the numbers being approximate distances in kilometres.

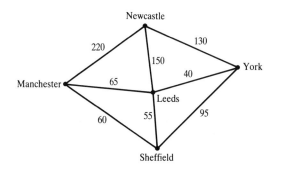

Imagine that these towns are to be linked by a cable TV system. The cables will run alongside roads, but all that is necessary is that all the towns are connected together. Two possibilities are:

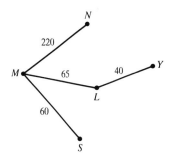

Total cable length 385 km   Total cable length reduced to 295 km

> **Draw a connecting system which has a smaller total length than either of the two illustrated above.**

You should have realised that the various possible connecting systems form **spanning trees.**

In practice, the cable company will want to use the shortest possible cable length in order to reduce the cost of setting up the system to a minimum, so this chapter will be concerned with finding **minimum spanning trees.**

You may be surprised to discover how many different spanning trees there can be for a fairly simple graph.

Two of the three possible spanning trees for the graph K_3 are shown below:

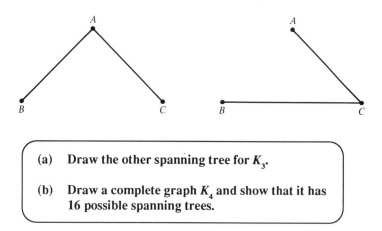

(a) Draw the other spanning tree for K_3.

(b) Draw a complete graph K_4 and show that it has 16 possible spanning trees.

The number of possible spanning trees increases very rapidly with the number of vertices in the graph. For K_{20} there are 2.6×10^{23} (more than a quarter of a million, million, million, million) trees. You will, of course, not always be dealing with complete graphs, but the number of possible trees can still be very high.

It would not be efficient, even if using a powerful computer, to list all the possible spanning trees in order to find the minimum one. It is preferable to develop a system of simple processes (or rules) which will lead to the minimum spanning tree.

(a) Draw a possible spanning tree for the points A to F and write down its length.

(b) Try to find a minimum spanning tree and write down its length. Discuss with other students the method you used to do it.

(c) Write down a series of rules which you think gives a minimum spanning tree and check that it works for a different set of points and distances.

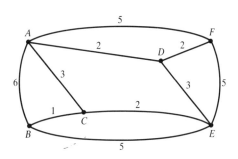

3.2 Prim's algorithm

In this chapter, two different procedures for finding a minimum spanning tree – Prim's and Kruskal's – will be considered and you may be interested to see if either of them is similar to yours.

Systematic procedures are often called **algorithms**. The word comes from the Latin translation (Algorismi) of the name of the 9th century Arab mathematician al-Khwarizmi.

Prim's algorithm

1   Choose any vertex to be the starting point of your tree, *T*.

2   Add to *T* the shortest remaining edge that has one end on *T* and one end not on *T*. (If there are two or more such edges choose one of them at random.)

3   Repeat step 2 until *T* contains all the necessary edges. (You should see why a network with *n* vertices will have a spanning tree with *n* – 1 edges.)

Notice that step 2 in the algorithm ensures that no circuits are formed.

Example 1

Use Prim's algorithm to obtain a minimum spanning tree for this graph.

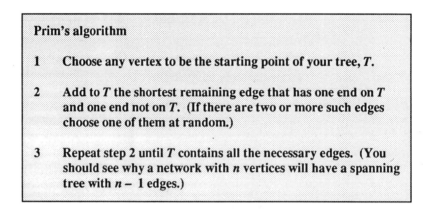

Solution

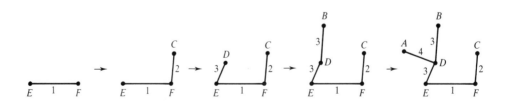

The tree has length 13 units.

Prim's algorithm is called a **greedy algorithm** because you always take the easiest (or 'greediest' route). Think of being 'greedy' to reach food quickly at the end of a walk!

The tree in Example 1 started with *EF*, the edge with the smallest possible length and this seems logical but in fact any starting point can be used.

> **Show that by starting at *A*, you can use Prim's algorithm to give you either the same spanning tree or a different one which also has length 13.**

Prim's algorithm will **always** produce a minimum spanning tree, but that tree may not be unique.

Example 2

The diagram shows possible connections between towns which are to be linked into a cable TV network. The numbers represents the cost of installing cable between the towns. Find the minimum cost of linking all of the towns by cable.

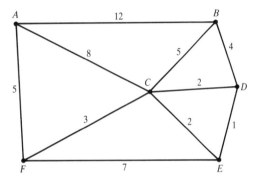

Solution

There are 6 towns to be linked and so 5 cable links are required. One possible minimum spanning tree is obtained as follows:

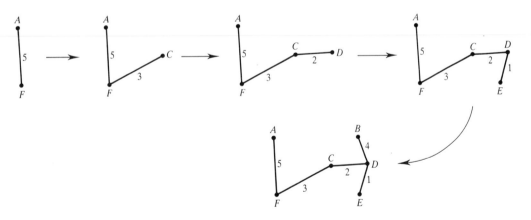

The minimum cost of installing the cable is 15 units.

Exercise 1

1 The diagram shows the positions of tents on a camp site, with the distances between them in metres. Work out how to link all the tents by paths so that the total length of pathway is minimum.

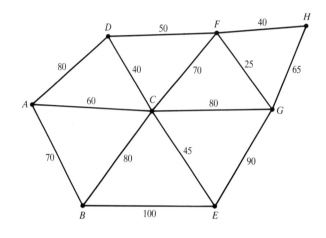

2 The towns shown below are to be joined by a cable network. Show how to do this using the smallest possible total length of cable. (The distances are in kilometres.)

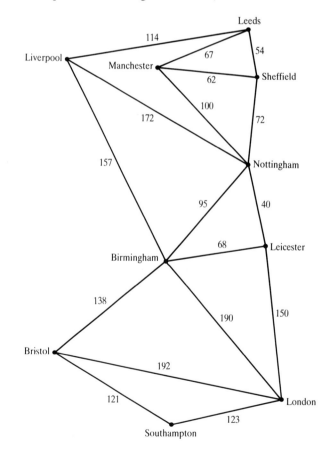

36

3.3 Computing with Prim's algorithm

You have no doubt realised that, even using Prim's algorithm, finding the minimum spanning tree for a large network would be time-consuming, and that the use of a computer would seem sensible. Indeed, algorithms have become particularly important in recent years because they can be translated relatively easily into computer programs.

In order to use a computer to find a minimum spanning tree, the first step would be to convert the network into a table. (Crosses in the table show that there is no link between the given points.)

The network   may be expressed as

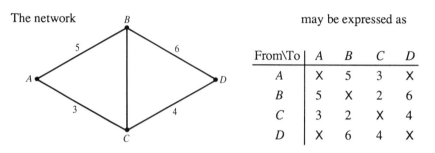

From\To	A	B	C	D
A	X	5	3	X
B	5	X	2	6
C	3	2	X	4
D	X	6	4	X

Suppose you decide to start the spanning tree at B. From the B row you can see that the shortest possible edge is BC.

In order to avoid the possibility of circuits forming, no further edges should **end** at B or C, so columns B and C are deleted from the table.

From\To	A	D
A	X	X
B	5	6
C	3	4
D	X	X

You can now build the tree from B or C, so select the minimum length which is left in either the B or the C row.
This is C to A, with length 3.

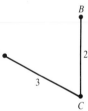

Now delete the A column and it is clear that the last link is from C to D, with length 4.

From\To	D
A	X
B	6
C	4
D	X

The spanning tree has a length of 9 units.

> **Repeat Example 1 using the procedure of this section.**

You may now like to try to write a program for Prim's algorithm – if so, you can use it in Exercise 2.

Exercise 2

1   The table represents a complete graph K_5.

From\To	A	B	C	D	E
A	X	10	8	7	10
B	10	X	5	4	9
C	8	5	X	7	10
D	7	4	7	X	8
E	10	9	10	8	X

(a)   How can you tell that it is a complete graph?

(b)   Find a minimum spanning tree for the graph.

2   An 18th century landscape garden has the following features:

Grotto (G), Cascade (C), Temple (T) and statues of
Bacchus (B), Diana (D), Hercules (H) and Venus (V).

The table shows the distances (in metres) between these features.

The new owners of the garden are about to open it to the public. They wish to construct the shortest possible length of pathway which will enable visitors to go to each of the features. What is this shortest possible length?

From\To	G	C	T	B	D	H	V
G	X	X	300	X	X	600	450
C	X	X	900	350	400	X	X
T	300	900	X	500	X	X	200
B	X	350	500	X	100	X	150
D	X	400	X	100	X	150	X
H	600	X	X	X	150	X	100
V	450	X	200	150	X	100	X

3.4   Kruskal's algorithm

The American mathematician Martin Kruskal has also developed an algorithm for
finding minimum spanning trees. His algorithm is also a 'greedy' one, since it works by
considering minimum distances. It is different from Prim's algorithm in that it works in
terms of edge lengths rather than by considering going from point to point.

Kruskal's algorithm

1   **Start with the shortest edge.**

2   **Choose the shortest edge remaining that does not complete a
     circuit with any of those already chosen. (If there is more
     than one possible choice, pick one at random.)**

3   **Repeat step 2 until you have chosen $n - 1$ edges (assuming
     that your network had n vertices).**

Example 3

Use Kruskal's algorithm to find the
minimum spanning tree for this
network.

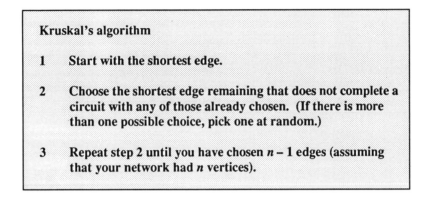

Solution

Start by linking C to D and then A to B.

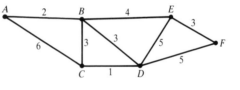

The next step could be B to C, B to D or E to F.

Choose B to C first.

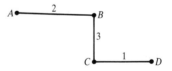

You should notice that there are still two edges of length 3 units left, but that one of
them cannot be used because it would form a circuit.

> **Explain clearly how to complete the solution. You should
> obtain a minimum spanning tree of length 13 units.**

Exercise 3 gives you a chance to decide whether you prefer Prim's or Kruskal's algorithm for the fairly simple problems which can be worked out quite quickly without a computer.

Tasksheet 1E looks at the early stages of writing a program for Kruskal's algorithm, so that you can begin to see whether one algorithm has advantages over the other when used for computer work. If you are interested in this aspect, answer only question 1 from Exercise 3 and then go on to Tasksheet 1E.

Exercise 3

1   The map shows a bird reserve. (A scrape is a lake with artificial islands on which birds nest.) The Wildlife Trust which runs the reserve wishes to construct wheel-chair paths so that disabled visitors can get to the Centre and all the hides. Use Kruskal's algorithm to advise them on the best way of doing this. All the possible paths (with costs of constructing them in hundreds of pounds) are given on the map.

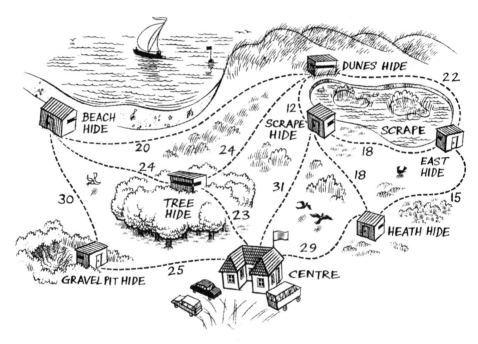

2   The reserve manager believes that it is not worth having a wheelchair path to the tree hide. How much money can be saved by leaving out this hide?

Show your working for this. You may like to draw a new map without the tree hide. Alternatively, you could draw up a table for the Centre and all the other hides and try to work out how to use Kruskal's algorithm from a table, as you did for Prim's algorithm in Section 3.3.

   TASKSHEET 1E – *Kruskal's algorithm*

After working through this chapter you should:

1 recognise problems which can be solved by finding a minimum spanning tree;

2 know how to find a minimum spanning tree using either Prim's or Kruskal's algorithm;

3 be aware of the fact that these algorithms can be used to enable lengthy problems to be solved using a computer.

Kruskal's algorithm

The aim in this tasksheet will be to work out how to use Kruskal's algorithm when working from information in tabular form.

1   Table 1 is taken from Exercise 2, where it was used to find a minimum spanning tree using Prim's algorithm. Kruskal's algorithm is about edges, rather than moving from point to point, so you may find it easier to work from Table 2. (It should be obvious that Tables 1 and 2 give the same information, provided that all paths can be travelled in either direction.)

       Try to find the minimum spanning tree from one of the tables using Kruskal's algorithm. Your main problem will be in working out how to avoid obtaining circuits.

       Write out clear directions for using Kruskal's algorithm when working from a table.

From\To	A	B	C	D	E
A	X	10	8	7	10
B	10	X	5	4	9
C	8	5	X	7	10
D	7	4	7	X	8
E	10	9	10	8	X

Table 1

From\To	A	B	C	D	E
A		10	8	7	10
B			5	4	9
C				7	10
D					8
E					

Table 2

2   Write the information about paths on the bird reserve from Exercise 3 in a suitable tabular form. Follow the directions written for question 1 and check that you obtain a minimum spanning tree of the same length as the one you obtained in Exercise 3.

3   In deciding which of the two algorithms would be preferable for computer use, two things needed to be considered – ease of programming and the time taken for the programs to run. What do you think are the advantages and disadvantages of the two algorithms in this respect.

4 Shortest paths

4.1 A greedy algorithm

Many problems in industry and commerce involve optimising resources, time, profits and so on. Using the concept of isomorphism, a problem of this type can often be solved mathematically using a weighted graph. The problem then becomes one of finding a shortest or longest path through the graph. You have already met such a problem in critical path analysis.

As an example, consider a map of shipping lanes between seven ports, the figures representing the estimated time (in days) between ports. The problem is to find the quickest route from A to G.

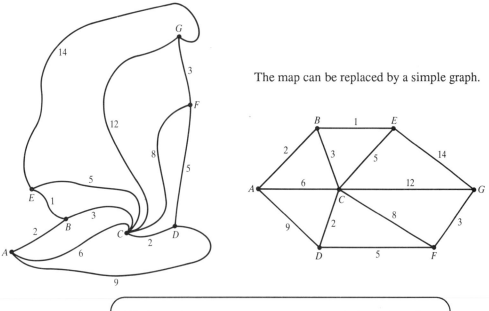

The map can be replaced by a simple graph.

> **Find the shortest path through the graph from A to G.**

Although you may have been able to solve the simple problem above by inspection, problems from industry require very large and involved networks for which computers are an essential aid. Optimising paths through such a network requires an algorithm or set of rules that can be programmed into a computer.

(a) For the graph above, trace a path from A to G, leaving each vertex by the edge with least weight. Does this 'greedy' algorithm give you the shortest path through the graph?

(b) Try to develop an algorithm that will give the shortest path. Try the algorithm out on a fellow student. Does it work?

4.2　Dynamic programming

This section and the following one introduce two algorithms that can be used to solve shortest path problems. You may already have invented an algorithm similar to one of these in the opening discussion point. The first algorithm is referred to as dynamic programming

Consider, once again, the shipping lanes problem.

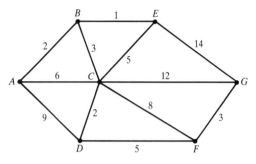

Step 1　Assign the value 0 to the starting vertex, A. Label the vertices which can be reached directly from the starting vertex as shown.

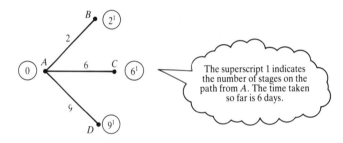

The superscript 1 indicates the number of stages on the path from A. The time taken so far is 6 days.

Step 2　Label any vertex which can be reached directly from a 1-stage vertex as shown.

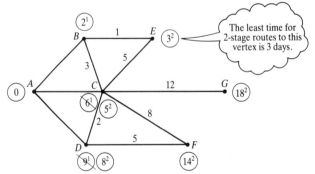

The least time for 2-stage routes to this vertex is 3 days.

Any vertex which has already been labelled is only relabelled if the total time is reduced. In this case, vertices C and D are relabelled.

Step 3　Repeat step 2 for 3-stage paths, then for 4-stage paths ... When no further improvement occurs, the optimal path has been found and can easily be retraced.

The dynamic programming algorithm builds up a set of **optimum** paths involving first 1-stage routes, then 2-stage routes, then 3-stage routes and so on, always leaving open the possibility that a path with more stages might be an improvement. When no further improvement occurs in the network, a **steady state** or **convergence** has been achieved.

Exercise 1

Use dynamic programming to solve the following problems.

1

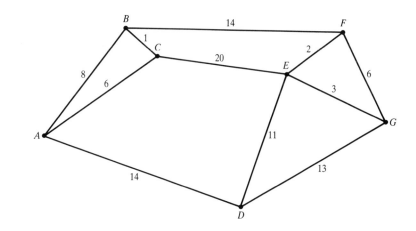

The graph represents land routes between two towns, A and G, in a mountainous region. The values represent the unit cost, in hundreds of pounds, of transportation along each section. Find the cheapest route from A to G.

When a graph has some or all of its edges directed, the dynamic programming algorithm is even easier to apply because fewer routes need to be considered.

2   Find the shortest time for a route from A to G if the shipping lane from D to C is one-way.

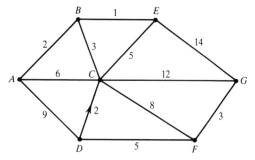

3   In the following graph find the shortest path from A to G.

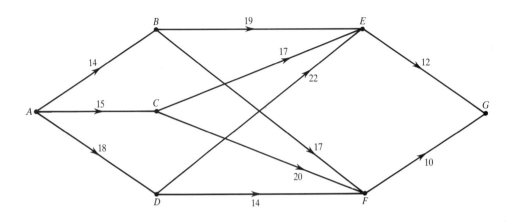

4   The diagram below illustrates the road system in an inner city. The values represent the estimated times, in minutes, over each section. Find the quickest route from A to J.

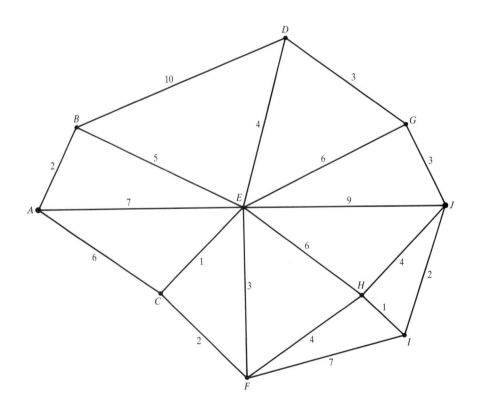

4.3   Dijkstra's algorithm

Again consider the shipping problem, this time using another method, called Dijkstra's algorithm, to find the shortest path.

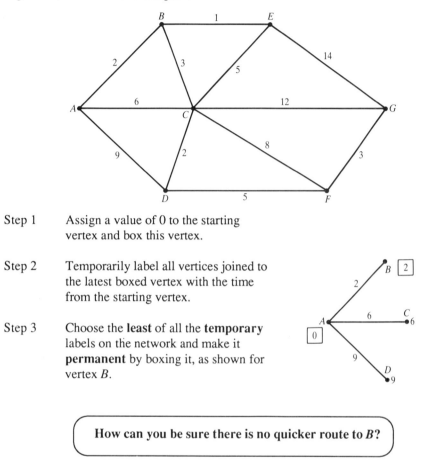

Step 1   Assign a value of 0 to the starting vertex and box this vertex.

Step 2   Temporarily label all vertices joined to the latest boxed vertex with the time from the starting vertex.

Step 3   Choose the **least** of all the **temporary** labels on the network and make it **permanent** by boxing it, as shown for vertex *B*.

> **How can you be sure there is no quicker route to *B*?**

Step 4   Repeat steps 2 and 3. If the path to a vertex with a temporary label is reduced on a subsequent step, use the reduced value, otherwise the label is unchanged.

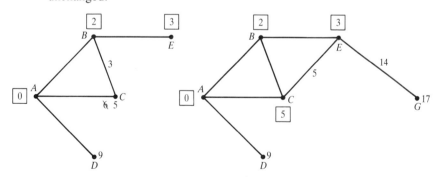

When the destination vertex has been boxed, the shortest path through the graph has been found and the path can easily be retraced.

You should have found that Dijkstra's algorithm is similar to dynamic programming in that you move through the graph choosing the shortest path in stages. The two algorithms will be looked at in more detail in the next section.

Exercise 2

Use Dijkstra's algorithm to solve the following questions.

1   The map below shows the distance in kilometres between various French towns. What is the shortest route from Tours to:

(a)   Bordeaux   (b)   Périgueux?

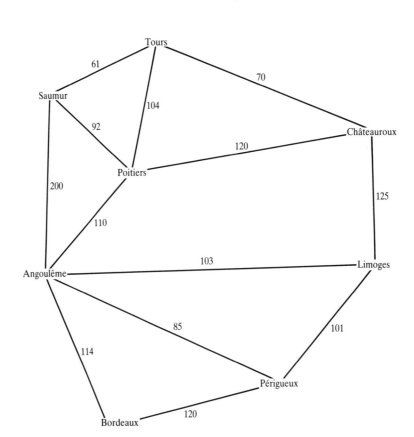

2   The graph below represents part of a one-way system in a city centre and shows the estimated times, in minutes, to travel each section. A dispatch rider wishes to get from *A* to *J* as quickly as possible. Advise on the best route.

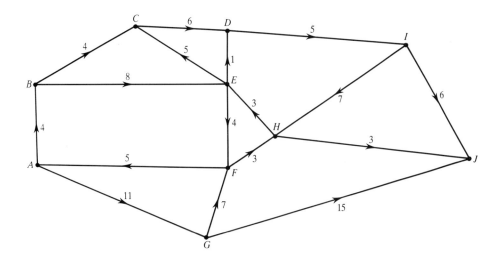

3   Often information is given in the form of a table rather than a graph. Adapt Dijkstra's algorithm to find the shortest path from Tours to Bordeax using the distance chart (in km) below. Check that your answer agrees with that to question 1(a).

From\To	T	S	Po	C	A	L	Pe	B
Tours	–	61	104	70	–	–	–	–
Saumur	61	–	92	–	200	–	–	–
Poitiers	104	92	–	120	110	–	–	–
Châteauroux	70	–	120	–	–	125	–	–
Angoulême	–	200	110	–	–	103	85	114
Limoges	–	–	–	125	103	–	101	–
Périgueux	–	–	–	–	85	101	–	120
Bordeaux	–	–	–	–	114	–	120	–

A blank (–) in the table indicates no direct route between two towns.

4.4 Choosing an algorithm

Both dynamic programming and Dijkstra's algorithm can be used to find the shortest path through the following graph.

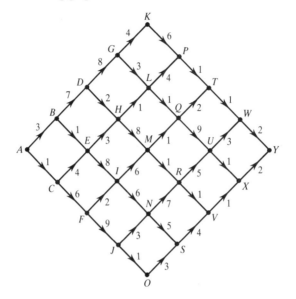

(a) Use both algorithms to find the shortest path through the above graph from A to Y.

(b) Explain why Dijkstra's algorithm is usually more efficient than dynamic programming in finding the shortest path through a graph.

 TASKSHEET 1 – *Longest paths and negative weighted graphs*

Dynamic programming and Dijkstra's algorithm will produce the shortest path through a positively weighted graph. As dynamic programming considers the shortest path to **every** vertex, Dijkstra's algorithm is usually more efficient, requiring fewer operations to find the shortest path.

When negative weighted edges are introduced into a problem or when the longest path through a graph is required, Dijkstra's algorithm cannot be used and so it is necessary to revert to dynamic programming.

The ability to find the longest path through a graph is particularly important when finding the **critical path** through a graph representing a complex scheduling of interrelated activities. The minimum time in which a project can be completed is dependent upon all the critical activities being completed on time. These critical activities will lie on the **longest path** through the graph.

Exercise 3

1   A parcel delivery service, based at *A*, is hired by a company to make regular
    deliveries to premises close to *B*, *C*, *D*, *E*, *F* and *G*. The company's warehouse is
    located along *CD* so vans using that section are able to collect the next batch of
    parcels without making a special journey. The figures on the graph represent the
    average cost, in £, incurred by the delivery service in making a delivery run along
    each section.

    (a)   Explain the negative value on the section *CD*.

    (b)   Recommend the routes that the delivery service should take to each
          delivery drop.

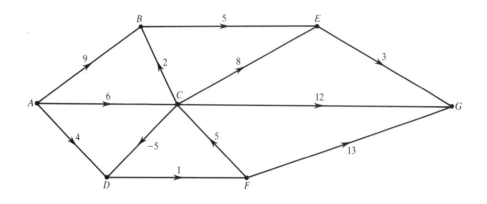

2   Find (a) the shortest path and (b) the longest path through the following graph
    from *A* to *I*.

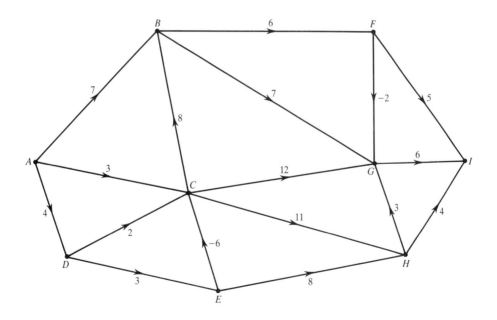

3   Find the shortest path from St. Louis to Washington.

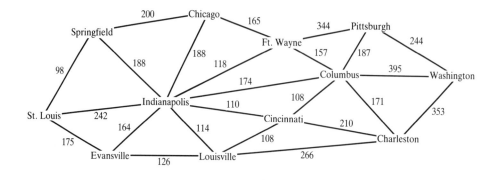

4   The following graph represents the scheduling of activities for a building contract. The value on each edge represents the estimated time (in weeks) for each of the activities to be completed.

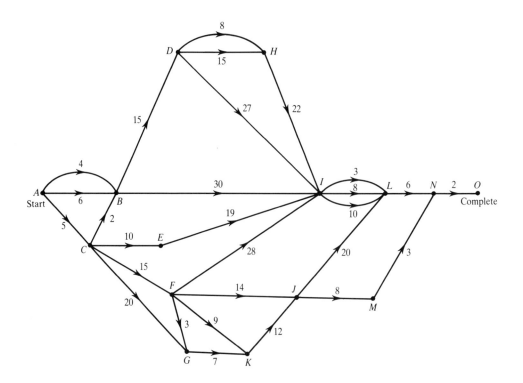

Find the critical path through the graph and give the shortest time in which the contract can be completed if the builder has sufficient resources to keep to schedule.

TASKSHEET 2E – *Operations*

After working through this chapter you should:

1   be aware of the wide range of problems that can be approached using an analysis of optimum paths through graphs;

2   be able to apply both dynamic programming and Dijkstra's algorithm to shortest path problems;

3   be aware of the limitations of Dijkstra's algorithm in solving certain categories of optimum path problems and the need to revert to the more general method of dynamic programming.

Longest paths and negative weightings

1

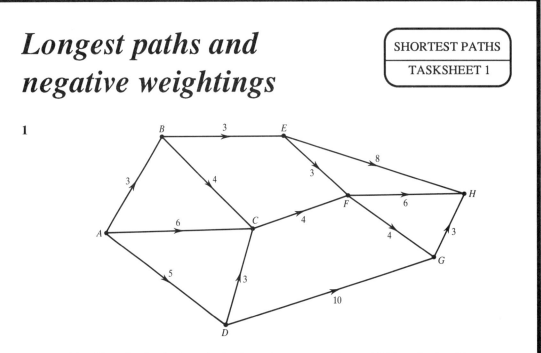

(a) Try adapting both methods, dynamic programming and Dijkstra's algorithm, to find the **longest path** through the graph from *A* to *G*. Explain why one method is successful and the other is not.

(b) Interpret the digraph and your value for the longest path in terms of a scheduling activity requiring a critical path.

All the graphs considered so far have involved positive weighted edges, but the economics of costs and profits to firms of certain activities may lead to an analysis involving negative weighted edges.

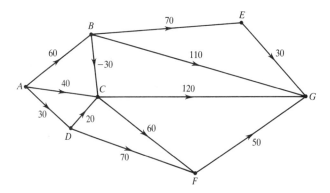

In the graph above, the positive weightings represent costs to a firm (in £) of certain activities and the negative weightings represent an action producing profit.

2

(a) Use dynamic programming to find the optimum path through the network from *A* to *G*. Now try Dijkstra's algorithm.

(b) Explain why Dijkstra's algorithm is unsuccessful for graphs with **negative edges.**

Operations

The efficiency of Dijkstra's algorithm and dynamic programming has already been touched upon in Section 4.4. Computers are essential tools in **Decision mathematics** when investigating network problems of a realistic scale. To reduce the computing time and make the problem manageable it is important to reduce the number of arithmetic operations (additions, subtractions, comparisons of two numbers) to a minimum.

Consider the most complicated graph involving six vertices – each vertex being connected to every other vertex.

In the thinking point of Section 4.2 you were asked to consider the maximum possible number of edges in a **path** through a graph consisting of n vertices.

1   What is the maximum number of edges in a path for the graph shown?

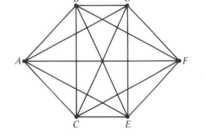

2   To find the shortest path from A to G through the graph shown, consider Dijkstra's algorithm. Assume initially that all the vertices are assigned the value zero. To reach vertices B, C, D, E and F from vertex A five additions are required, zero plus the weighting on each edge.

(a)   How many comparisons are required to label each vertex temporarily after just one stage of the path?

(b)   How many comparisons are required to box one of these temporary labels and make it permanent?

(c)   How many vertices need to be considered when finding the second stage (edge) of the path?

Length of path	No. of vertices to consider	No. of additions	No. of comparisons
1	5	5	5 + 4
2	4		
3			
4			
5			

(d)   Complete the table and calculate the total number of operations required to find the shortest path from A to F.

(continued)

55

(e)   Consider the same problem but for a graph with n vertices:

    (i)   find the maximum number of additions required;

    (ii)   find the maximum number of comparisons required;

    (iii) show that the total for the maximum number of operations required is given by the formula $1.5n^2 - 2.5n + 1$.

3   Dynamic programming can also be used to find the shortest path from A to F for the graph shown, but this time vertices are not dropped from consideration as you move through the problem. At each stage, each vertex must be considered and updated if a shorter route is found.

Assigning zero to vertex A, all the vertices B to F can be approached by 1-stage paths from vertex A, involving a total of five additions.

(a)   Explain why no comparisons are required at this stage.

At successive stages of the calculations you will need to consider approaching each vertex via another vertex in the graph which is already accessible. Vertex B can be approached by 2-stage paths, or less, from all the other five vertices, resulting in five additions.

(b)   How many comparisons are required to label B after considering 2-stage paths or less?

(c)   How many additions and comparisons are required to label vertex C after considering 2-stage paths or less?

(d)   What is the total number of additions and comparisons required to label all the vertices B, C, D, E and F after considering 2-stage paths or less?

Length of path	No. of vertices to consider	No. of additions	No. of comparisons
1	6	5	0
2 or less	6	5×5	4×5
3 or less	6	5×5	
4 or less	6		
5 or less	6		

(e)   Complete the table by considering first 3-stage paths or less to each vertex, 4-stage paths or less to each vertex and so on. Calculate the total number of operations required in finding the shortest path from A to F.

(continued)

(f)   Consider the same problem but for a graph with n vertices:

   (i)   find the maximum number of additions required;

   (ii)   find the maximum number of comparisons required;

   (iii)   show that the total for the maximum number of operations is given by the formula $2n^3 - 9n^2 + 14n - 7$.

4   Investigate the maximum number of operations required to find the shortest path through graphs, with increasing numbers of vertices, using Dijkstra's algorithm and dynamic programming.

(a)   Which is the more efficient algorithm?

(b)   Use the formulas from questions 1 and 2 to explain your answer to part (a).

5 Line inspection

5.1   The Chinese postman problem

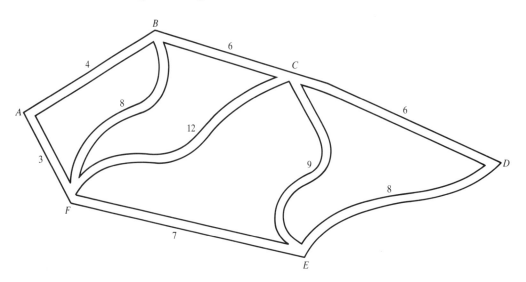

A street network
(distances in tens of metres)

A postman is to deliver letters along all the streets shown and return to the start point.

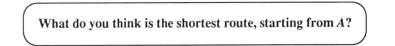

What do you think is the shortest route, starting from *A*?

Problems such as this were first analysed by the Chinese mathematician Mei-ko Kwan, hence the name of this section.

Mei-ko Kwan reasoned as follows:

•   Such a tour can be made without repeating a street if, and only if, all the vertices are even. (See Section 2.1 *The Konigsberg bridges*)

•   The only edges in the graph are those shown; new 'streets' cannot be added.

•   If there are odd vertices, all the vertices must be made even by retracing steps – that is by repeating edges.

Following this line of reasoning the problem given can be solved methodically. *B* and *E* are the only odd vertices. They must be made even by repeating edges. The edges to repeat are those giving the shortest distance between *B* and *E*, namely *BA*, *AF* and *FE*. The result is the multiply-connected weighted graph given on the next page.

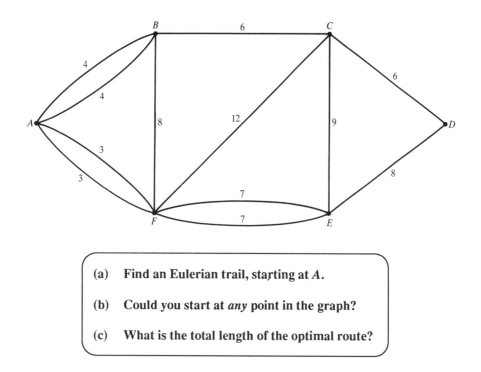

(a) Find an Eulerian trail, starting at A.

(b) Could you start at *any* point in the graph?

(c) What is the total length of the optimal route?

Thinking of graphs with more than two odd vertices, Mei-ko Kwan recalled an important result concerning the orders of the vertices of any graph.

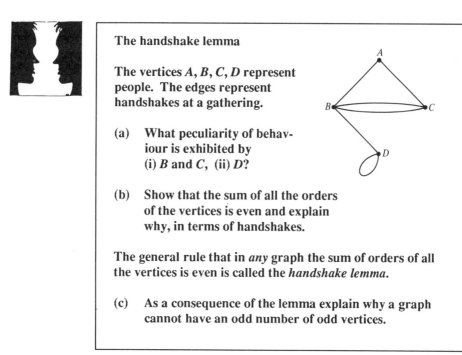

The handshake lemma

The vertices A, B, C, D represent people. The edges represent handshakes at a gathering.

(a) What peculiarity of behaviour is exhibited by
(i) B and C, (ii) D?

(b) Show that the sum of all the orders of the vertices is even and explain why, in terms of handshakes.

The general rule that in *any* graph the sum of orders of all the vertices is even is called the *handshake lemma*.

(c) As a consequence of the lemma explain why a graph cannot have an odd number of odd vertices.

The fact that there will always be an even number of odd vertices means that such vertices can be paired off. For each pairing, the shortest distances between pairs of odd vertices can then be found; in this way the optimal pairing is discovered. Finally, when all the vertices have been 'made even' in the optimal way there is an easy algorithm for finding an Eulerian trail.

 TASKSHEET 1 – *Fleury's algorithm*

The Chinese postman algorithm

To solve the Chinese postman problem for a given weighted graph:

- **find the odd vertices;**

- **pair off these vertices so that the sum of shortest distances between pairs of vertices is least;**

- **add in the edges of these shortest distances to form a multiply-connected graph with even vertices;**

- **find an Eulerian trail, either by inspection or using Fleury's algorithm.**

Despite its traditional name, in practice the algorithm is used most to solve problems involving inspections of networks of various kinds, in order to find faults in need of correction. A modern application of the algorithm of great economic importance is in the checking of printed circuits. These electrical networks have very large numbers of vertices and it is highly desirable that the linking edges should all be tested for continuity and uniformity.

Think of three other kinds of network requiring such inspections.

Exercise 1

1

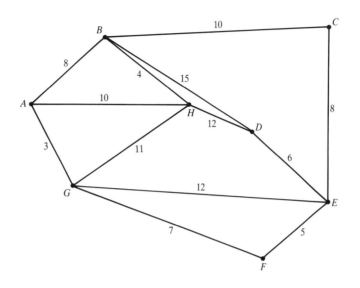

*A street network
(distances in tens of metres)*

This street network is to be patrolled by a policeman 'on the beat'. What is the length of his optimal route?

2   (a)   For the given network show that there are four odd vertices which can be paired off in three different ways.

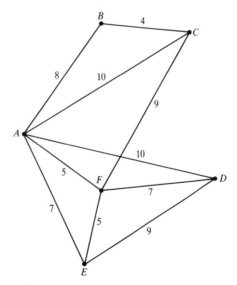

(b)   For each of the three ways find the sum of the shortest distances between pairs of odd vertices. Hence find the length of the optimal 'Chinese postman' route around the network.

5.2　The travelling salesperson's problem

You have seen that line inspection involves traversing all the **edges** of a weighted graph. A companion problem is to visit all its **vertices** by an optimal route. Taking vertices as towns and edges as roads (or rail or air routes) this is the sort of problem facing a sales representative. Hence the task of finding such a tour is known classically as the travelling salesperson's problem. Strangely, whereas there is a satisfactory algorithm for the Chinese postman's problem, no easy solution has been found for the travelling salesperson's.

An obvious algorithm is to find and compare all possible tours. For a complete graph with n vertices this would mean considering $(n - 1)!$ tours.

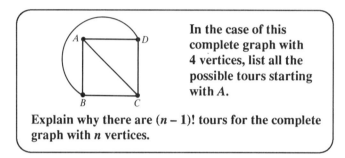

In the case of this complete graph with 4 vertices, list all the possible tours starting with A.

Explain why there are $(n - 1)!$ tours for the complete graph with n vertices.

For each of the $(n - 1)!$ tours n additions would be needed, giving a total of $n \times (n - 1)! = n!$ additions. Besides all these additions a large number of comparisons would have to be made. For a graph with n vertices a problem whose solution by computer requires a time proportional to some exponential a^n $(a > 1)$ or to $n!$ is classified as 'hard'. When n is large the algorithm described would not be feasible in practice.

How long would it take a computer performing 100 000 additions each second to make 20! additions?

Practical problems of the salesperson's tour type often involve very large numbers of vertices. For example, in the manufacture of printed circuit boards one task is to drill a number of holes. Each board may require many thousands or even hundreds of thousands of holes. Though an optimal route for the laser drill is not normally feasible, some method of producing a reasonable route fairly quickly is desirable.

5.3 The nearest neighbour algorithm

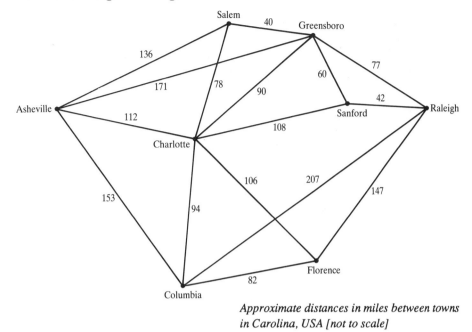

*Approximate distances in miles between towns
in Carolina, USA [not to scale]*

Marylou is a sales representative in Columbia, South Carolina. She uses a mileage chart
to plan a helicopter trip taking in the cities shown, in a round tour. The algorithm she
tries is a 'greedy' one, in which at each stage the next city is the closest not previously
visited. Using this 'nearest neighbour' rule the first stage of the tour will be Columbia –
Florence.

> **Describe what happens if she continues to apply the
> nearest neighbour algorithm. Modify the algorithm
> to plan what you consider a reasonable tour.**

As a result of her calculations Marylou settles on the following route:

Columbia – Florence – Charlotte – Sanford – Raleigh –
Greensboro – Salem – Asheville – Columbia

giving a total distance of:

82 + 106 + 108 + 42 + 77 + 40 + 136 + 153 = 744 miles

Later, she mentions her problem to Yvette, a colleague. Yvette points out that the tour
takes in all the cities so it will look the same whichever start point is chosen.

> **Apply the nearest neighbour algorithm starting at Charlotte.**

Now Marylou feels that she may have solved the problem. By applying the nearest neighbour algorithm starting from each town in turn, she hopes to find the optimal solution, but if she thinks this method is certain to work in every case, she is doomed to disappointment.

 TASKSHEET 2 – *Planning a sales tour*

However, Marylou's method is one found useful in determining near-optimal routes by computer.

> **There is no known algorithm which guarantees an 'easy' solution of the travelling salesperson's problem.**

Exercise 2

1   Find which starting city gives Marylou her shortest mileage, using the nearest neighbour algorithm.

2

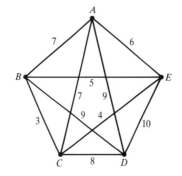

Use the nearest neighbour algorithm starting with each of the five cities A, B, C, D and E. Do you think you have found an optimal route?

3   A hygiene inspector lives in town A and has to visit restaurants in towns $B–F$. Use the nearest neighbour algorithm to recommend a route.

	A	B	C	D	E	F
A	–	16	13	11	7	8
B	16	–	10	5	12	10
C	13	10	–	4	7	9
D	11	5	4	–	6	7
E	7	12	7	6	–	9
F	8	10	9	7	9	–

5.4   Heuristic methods

It has been stressed that, as the salesperson's tour problem is hard, in practice an optimal solution may not be expected. The search for an acceptable near-optimal solution may then be conducted in two phases:

* a selection of a trial start tour;
* local improvements.

This 'trial and improvement' approach will be familiar to you, for example in finding approximate roots of equations. In computing, such a technique is called a **heuristic**.

In principle, the start tour could be chosen at random but where possible it will be made as nearly 'circular' as possible. It could be found by Marylou's method, based on the 'nearest unvisited city' algorithm, which is itself a heuristic approach. Then local improvements may be made using the so called **2-optimal** method. Stages in this process are shown below.

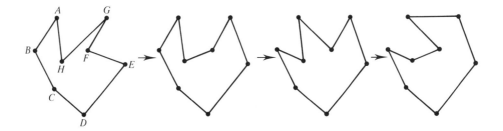

In the first step, cuts have been made in edges *GH* and *FE* and vertices rejoined to form an improved tour.

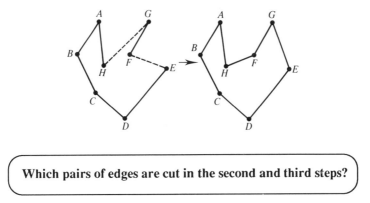

> **Which pairs of edges are cut in the second and third steps?**

In the algorithm based on the 2-optimal method, a new tour is kept only when it is an improvement on the one replaced. The procedure is repeated either a prescribed number of times or until no improvement results a certain number of times in succession.

A '3-optimal' method, involving the cutting of three edges and subsequent reconnection, has also been programmed. Further details of heuristic methods may be found in articles in *New Scientist* (14 April 1990 and 12 December 1992).

5.5 Upper and lower bounds

Although the salesperson's problem can at present be solved only by extensive (and expensive) 'number crunching' there are simple (and technically 'easy') methods of finding bounds for the 'least distance'. These bounds may be useful in arriving quickly at a rough estimate of the optimal distance.

Any answer found by considering a particular tour is, of course, an upper bound. For example, Marylou's distance of 742 miles is an upper bound for the tour of Carolina cities. There is always the chance that a tour found by inspection or by using the nearest neighbour algorithm will be optimal (that is, a **least** upper bound).

Finding a minimum connector is a particularly easy process and so it is often used in fixing bounds. The upper bound found by this method is likely to be very crude. First a minimum connector is found for the cities. Then a complete tour, providing an upper bound, is made by traversing each edge (flying along each link) both ways, as shown in the diagram below.

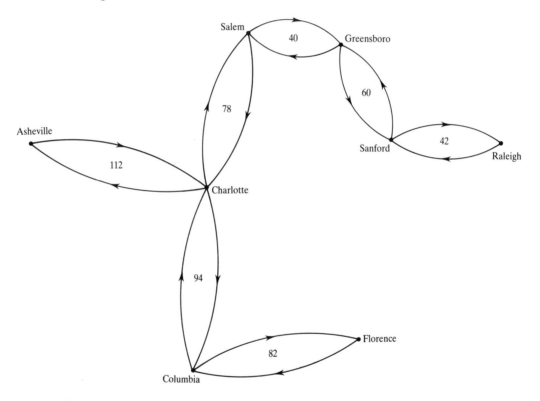

Columbia – Florence – Columbia – Charlotte – Asheville – Charlotte – Salem – Greensboro – Sanford – Raleigh – Sanford – Greensboro – Salem – Charlotte – Columbia is a possible tour, of length 2 x (40 + 60 + 42 + 78 + 94 + 82 + 112) = 1016 miles. So 1016 is an upper bound for the optimum mileage.

A minimum connector can also be used to find a lower bound but in this case the idea is more difficult to follow.

The optimal tour will form a circuit, say *PQRSTUP*.

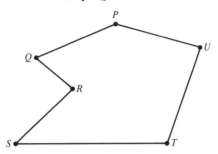

Imagine one vertex, for example *U*, detached from this circuit.

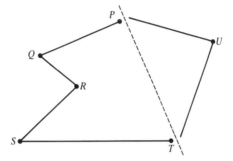

The section P, Q, R, S, T on the left forms a tree so the total length of its edges must be greater than or equal to the length of the minimum spanning tree connecting P, Q, R, S and T. (Note that this **minimum spanning tree** (MST) may be branching, rather than linear.)

The section on the right, consisting of two edges only, must have length greater than or equal to the two shortest edges incident on U.

So the total length of the optimal tour must be greater than or equal to the length of:

MST for $\{P, Q, R, S, T\}$ + two shortest edges from U.

To find a lower bound of the length of the optimal tour in the travelling salesperson's (TSP) problem :

- delete any vertex *V*;
- construct the minimum connector of the remaining vertices;
- add in the two shortest edges incident on *V*.

(It may be noted that in general the result is not a tour.)

For any given weighted graph, the method described gives a set of lower bounds, one for each of the vertices chosen as *V*.

Exercise 3

1 (a) By constructing the minimum connector for this graph find an upper bound for the length of the optimal salesperson's tour.

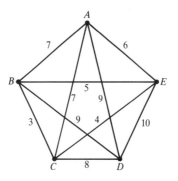

(b) Delete each vertex in turn and use the procedure above to find five lower bounds.

2 A van sets out from A to deliver spares to garages in towns B, C, D, E and F before returning to A. Calculate an upper bound for the optimal distance to be travelled. Use the procedure above to find the greatest of six lower bounds.

	A	B	C	D	E	F
A	–	9	12	5	4	7
B	9	–	7	3	14	9
C	12	7	–	6	12	5
D	5	3	6	–	13	17
E	4	14	12	13	–	4
F	7	9	5	17	4	–

3E Suppose that the procedure described at the end of this section results in a tour. Explain why this is a sufficient but not a necessary condition for optimality.

5.6   Scheduling

In attempting to solve the travelling salesperson's problem you have been seeking an optimum tour within a variety of route networks.

Similar problems also occur in situations not connected with journeys, such as in scheduling a series of activities, where the weights on the network may represent set-up times.

One such situation is used here to introduce an alternative method for finding a lower bound.

Example 1

A single machine is used to produce five chemicals, A, B, C, D and E. The table below gives the times in minutes needed to clear and reset the machine between the processes.

From\To	A	B	C	D	E
A	–	100	90	80	130
B	100	–	30	40	60
C	90	30	–	50	120
D	80	40	50	–	70
E	130	60	120	70	–

The manager wishes to plan a complete cycle (using each process once and returning to the start) which has the lowest possible total changeover time.

> (a)   Sketch a network to illustrate the information.
>
> (b)   Use the nearest neighbour algorithm starting from A to find one possible cycle which might provide an acceptable solution.
>
> (c)   Copy the table of values and ring the items you chose, commenting on the pattern formed by the rings.

You may have already noticed that the nearest neighbour algorithm can be used on the table without reference to the sketch. This makes the search for the best production schedule easier to program for a computer.

The problem of finding an optimum cycle may be regarded as a selection of one item from each row and column of the matrix to give the lowest possible total.

69

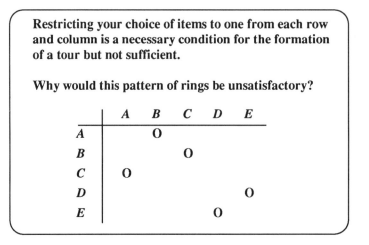

Restricting your choice of items to one from each row and column is a necessary condition for the formation of a tour but not sufficient.

Why would this pattern of rings be unsatisfactory?

	A	B	C	D	E
A		O			
B			O		
C	O				
D					O
E			O		

Regarding the problem in this way you can quickly establish a lower bound for the optimum tour.

In the table above one item must be selected from each row and column so that each chemical has a 'from' and 'to' link.

In the first row (from A), whichever number is chosen you can see that it must be greater than or equal to 80.

Similarly, for row B the number chosen ≥ 30,
for row C the number chosen ≥ 30,
for row D the number chosen ≥ 40,
for row E the number chosen ≥ 60.

So for any five numbers chosen one from each row, the total will certainly be greater than $(80 + 30 + 30 + 40 + 60) = 240$.

Subtracting the row minimum, the table can be adjusted to show the actual choice in row A more clearly as:

From\To	A	B	C	D	E	Minimum
		20	10	0	50	
A	•	1̶0̶0̶	9̶0̶	8̶0̶	1̶3̶0̶	(80)

This tells you that from row A at least 80 must be chosen, but 20, 10, 0 or 50 will be added to this, depending on which item you actually decide to select.

Make a copy of the table and adjust the values for rows B, C, D and E in a similar way.

Working now with your **adjusted values**, observe that when making the final choice, one item has to be selected from each column. Note the least value in each column.

70

For column A, the number chosen must be at least 40.
For columns B, C and D the number is at least 0.
For column E the number is at least 30.

That is, the numbers chosen, one from each column of adjusted values, must total at least $40 + 30 = 70$.

Any tour which consists of a choice of one item from each row and column of the original table of values must have a total length greater than $240 + 70 = 310$.

The manager cannot possibly find a production cycle taking less than 310 minutes.

Subtracting the column minima gives the final 'reduced matrix'.

From\To	A	B	C	D	E	Row min.
A	–	20	10	0	20 / ~~50~~	(80)
B	30 / ~~70~~	–	0	10	0 / ~~30~~	(30)
C	20 / ~~60~~	0	–	20	60 / ~~90~~	(30)
D	0 / ~~40~~	0	10	–	0 / ~~30~~	(40)
E	30 / ~~70~~	0	60	10	–	(60)
Col. min.	(40)	(0)	(0)	(0)	(30)	

Lower bound = Σ row minima + Σ column minima (reduced matrix) = 310

To summarise:

> **To find a lower bound from the table of values:**
>
> (i)   in each row find the minimum value, and subtract this from all entries in that row;
>
> (ii)   then for each column of *adjusted values* find the minimum value and subtract from all entries in that column;
>
> (iii) the sum of all row and column minima gives a lower bound for all tours.

This method is sometimes useful as an alternative to the method of finding a lower bound using spanning trees. In particular, the method may be used to find a lower bound even if the matrix is not symmetric. Such a situation might arise in paint production for example, when the changeover time from white to red, say, might not be the same as the changeover time from red to white.

Notice that an optimal tour has not yet been found. This would be done by going on to select items from the reduced matrix to give the lowest possible total.

Such a procedure is the essence of a class of approaches to the solution of the travelling salesperson's problem known as **branch and bound** methods. They depend on the idea of systematically constructing possible tours, testing the effect of including each of the zero items in the reduced matrix. In certain circumstances such methods may quickly provide an optimum solution but in others they may require an unacceptably large number of calculations and comparisons.

To explore these methods in depth is beyond the scope of the present course but the scheduling problem may be taken a little further.

You have seen that any tour will have length 310 + a choice from the final reduced matrix of one suitable item from each row and column.

If you can choose **all** these items to be zero then, of course, you will have an optimum solution. However, this may not be possible.

(a) **For example, if the decision is made to include *CB*, *BE* and *AD*, which are all zero in the reduced table, what other choices must be made for the two remaining items?**

(b) **What is the overall total in this case?**

(c) **Is this better than totals you can find using the nearest neighbour method with different starting points?**

(d) **You may like to try some other combinations of zero items.**

Exercise 4

1   A machine used in the production of dyes is used for batches of six different colours. These are produced in rotation but the machine must be flushed out between colours. The times in minutes required for each cleaning period are given in the table.

From\To	Black	White	Red	Blue	Yellow	Green
Black	–	40	30	25	35	30
White	10	–	15	15	20	35
Red	10	35	–	20	25	24
Blue	10	30	20	–	30	15
Yellow	10	25	12	20	–	20
Green	10	30	24	15	25	–

(a)   It is hoped to devise a sequence of operations which will use each colour once and return to the beginning of the cycle with a total cleaning time of less than 2 hours. Use the nearest neighbour algorithm to find a satisfactory solution.

(b)   The foreman thinks that it should be possible to find a cycle with a total cleaning time of under 100 minutes. Explain why this is impossible, showing all your calculations.

72

After working through this chapter you should:

1   understand why a graph always has an even number of odd vertices;

2   be able to apply an algorithm to solve the Chinese postman problem for small networks;

3   appreciate the practical importance of the algorithm in network inspection;

4   understand what is meant by the statement that the travelling salesperson's problem (TSP) is 'hard';

5   be able to use the nearest neighbour algorithm for the TSP problem;

6   understand the phrase 'a 2-optimal heuristic method';

7   be able to find upper and lower bounds for the optimal TSP route based on minimum spanning trees;

8   be able to tackle the TSP problem directly from a table of weights, and appreciate that the weights need not be distances;

9   appreciate the practical importance of finding near-optimal solutions to the TSP problem.

Fleury's algorithm

When, in a connected graph, all the vertices are of even order, then Fleury's algorithm provides an easy and systematic method of constructing an Eulerian trail. The only new idea involved is that of a **bridge**.

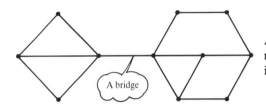

A bridge is an edge whose removal divides a connected graph into two disconnected parts.

The algorithm

(a)   Start at any vertex.

(b)   Traverse the edges in arbitrary order subject to these two rules:

    (i)   After each edge is traversed it is erased, together with any isolated vertex left behind.

    (ii)   At each stage a bridge can be traversed only if there is no alternative.

1   Apply the algorithm to these graphs. Write down the Eulerian trail obtained in each case.

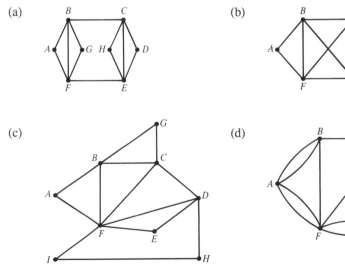

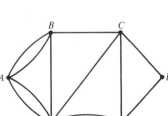

2   Explain why Fleury's algorithm works.

Planning a sales tour

A computer salesman has been allocated a new area and is planning his shortest sales tour. He has been given a table of distances in miles between the four towns in his patch.

From\To	A	B	C	D
A	–	60	70	90
B	60	–	35	50
C	70	35	–	55
D	90	50	55	–

From this table he feels it should be fairly easy to select the shortest tour, starting from his home base at Ashfield (*A*). He observes that the tour will consist of four legs, one to be chosen from each column.

He decides to imagine starting out from *A*, visiting the **nearest** neighbouring town and then to continue using the **shortest** link available.

1 Try this and note down the circuit obtained and its total length.

He wonders whether a different result might be obtained by choosing another starting point.

2 Try starting from *B*, from *C* and from *D* and in each case note down the circuit obtained and its length.

At this point the salesman imagines that he must have found the shortest tour. In fact, he has not.

3 Sketch a map showing the relative positions of *A*, *B*, *C* and *D*.

4 Hence find the optimal tour.

5 What would be the optimal tour if 25 replaced 35 for the length of *BC*?

Miscellaneous exercise

1   Some students have decided to spring clean a room in the house of a friend who is about to come out of hospital. The following activities are necessary:

    A – Remove curtains and take to cleaners ($\frac{1}{2}$ hour)
    B – Leave curtains at cleaners (6 hours)
    C – Collect curtains and buy flowers ($\frac{1}{2}$ hour)
    D – Move lighter furniture into another room ($\frac{1}{4}$ hour)
    E – Clean upholstery on removed furniture (1 hour)
    F – Polish wood on removed furniture ($\frac{1}{2}$ hour)
    G – Shampoo carpet (1 hour)
    H – Leave carpet to dry (5 hours)
    I – Hoover dry carpet ($\frac{1}{4}$ hour)
    J – Put up curtains and move back furniture ($\frac{1}{2}$ hour)
    K – Dust fittings and arrange flowers ($\frac{1}{4}$ hour)

    (a) Construct an activity table for the cleaning. Remember that you do not have to stand and watch the carpet dry, but you should not walk on a carpet in between the shampooing and the hoovering!

    (b) Draw a network diagram for the spring clean and use it to estimate the latest possible starting time if the room has to be ready for 5 p.m.

2   (a) A connected graph has n vertices. How many edges does a spanning tree have?

    (b) A connected graph G with 6 vertices has edges with 'lengths' 8, 7, 7, 5, 4, 4, 3, 3 and 3.

        (i)   What is the least possible length of a minimum spanning tree?

        (ii) Why might this length be impossible?

        (iii) Draw G in such a way that a minimum spanning tree has length 19.

3   How many spanning trees does this graph have?

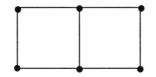

77

4   The map below shows part of the University of London Central Precinct. A motorist
wishes to get from Euston Square tube station (A) to the corner of Tavistock square (Q)
during the rush hour. From past experience she can estimate the journey time, in minutes,
along each section of road. These times are shown on the graph.

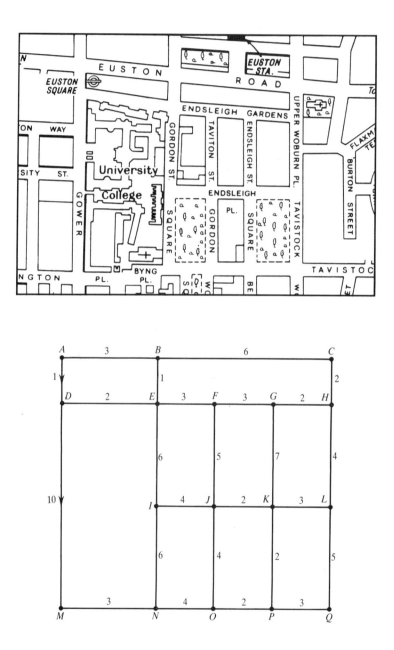

(a)   Which is the quickest route from A to Q?

(b)   Taviton Street is closed for major road works. What advice would you give to the
motorist?

5   (a)   Draw a digraph with the following vertex–vertex table.

	A	B	C	D	E
A	0	1	0	1	0
B	0	0	1	0	1
C	0	0	0	0	0
D	0	1	1	0	0
E	1	0	0	1	0

(b)   Sociologists sometimes represent relationships using digraphs. Use a digraph to show this information:

Ahmed likes Cheryl and Errol; Bettina likes Diana;
Cheryl likes Ahmed, Bettina and Errol; Diana likes
Bettina and Cheryl; Errol likes everybody.

6   In the following graph find the shortest **path** from A to E.

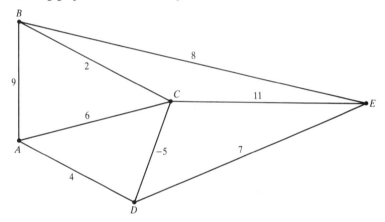

Explain why Dijkstra's algorithm does not necessarily give the optimum solution.

7   The following graph represents the expected profits (in £) on different stages of a proposed sales trip, starting from a home base at A and finishing at head office G. Find which route gives the maximum profit.

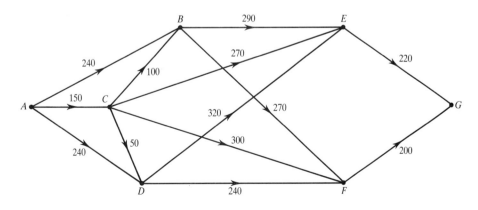

79

8 Find the shortest path from Manchester to London using the distance chart (in km) below.

From\To	M	S	Bi	N	Br	O	C	L
Manchester	–	61	130	–	–	–	–	–
Sheffield	61	–	–	61	–	–	–	–
Birmingham	130	–	–	79	142	101	–	–
Nottingham	–	61	79	–	–	153	135	198
Bristol	–	–	142	–	–	113	–	183
Oxford	–	–	101	153	113	–	–	90
Cambridge	–	–	–	135	–	–	–	89
London	–	–	–	198	183	90	89	–

A blank (–) in the table indicates no direct route between two towns.

9 A factory produces ice cream in five flavours using the same equipment for each. The flavours are produced in sequence and at each changeover a slightly different cleaning operation takes place. The times (in minutes) required for each changeover are as follows:

From\To	Vanilla	Strawberry	Raspberry	Peppermint	Lemon
Vanilla	–	8	9	10	10
Strawberry	15	–	10	12	10
Raspberry	15	10	–	8	9
Peppermint	25	22	20	–	18
Lemon	30	25	25	15	–

The manager wishes to produce the five flavours in a cycle requiring the minimum total changeover time.

(a) Sketch a network to illustrate all possible sequences of operation.

(b) Using an appropriate heuristic, find a suitable sequence of operations.

10 Euler's formula for a connected plane graph with v vertices, e edges and f faces is $v - e + f = 2$. Assuming this formula, find and justify a formula for plane graphs consisting of n disconnected parts.

11   The following graph represents the scheduling of activities for a manufacturing process. The values on each edge represent the time (in hours) for each of the activities to be completed.

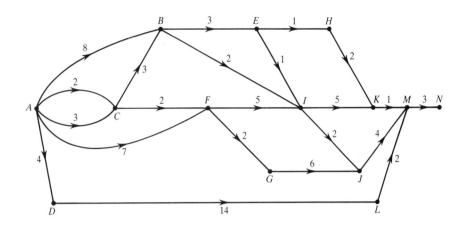

Find the critical path through the graph and hence the minimum time required to complete the process assuming sufficient resources are available.

12   The shape shown below is made up of right-angled triangles with edges of lengths 1, 1 and $\sqrt{2}$ units.

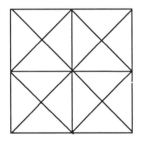

Consider this to be a graph with 13 vertices and 28 edges. What is the length of a minimal spanning tree?

13   (a)   The graph shown is the complete bipartite graph $K_{2,4}$. Show by drawing that $K_{2,4}$ is planar.

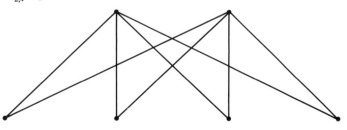

(b)   Generalise the result in part (a).

14 The network diagram shows the stages in a manufacturing process, with the time in hours for each stage.

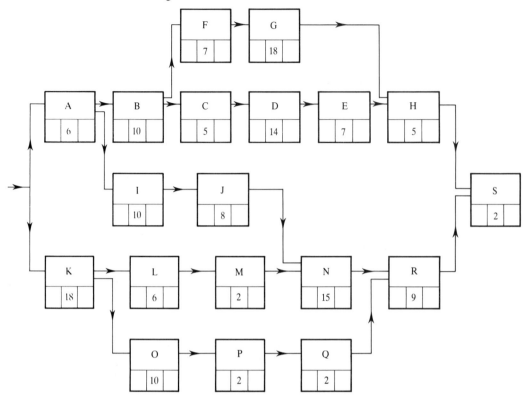

(a) On a copy of the diagram, write in the earliest start time for each stage and show that the minimum time for the complete process is 52 hours.

(b) On your diagram, write in the latest finish time for each stage and so mark the critical path.

(c) What is the float time for:

    (i)   stage P

    (ii)   stage G?

(d) It is possible to ensure that the whole process can be carried out by four workers. Draw a Gantt chart to show how this can be arranged. (You can assume that any worker can carry out any stage.)

(e) Draw the resources diagram corresponding to your Gantt chart.

15　In this road network, all distances are in kilometres.

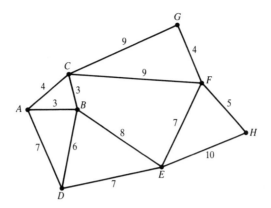

All the roads need to be cleared by a snow plough.

(a)　Is it possible for the snow plough to travel along each road exactly once and return to its starting point? Explain.

(b)　Suggest a route for the snow clearing operation and state the minimum total distance to be travelled.

(c)　The highway authority proposes to lay a new experimental road surface which is said to be resistant to icing on certain roads. The cost of the new surface is proportional to distance. Find a set of roads which will provide a connection between the towns at minimum cost. What is the total length of road to be resurfaced?

(d)　Use the results in (c) to state an upper bound for a tour visiting all the towns at least once.

16　Find the shortest path from A to P in each of the following graphs.

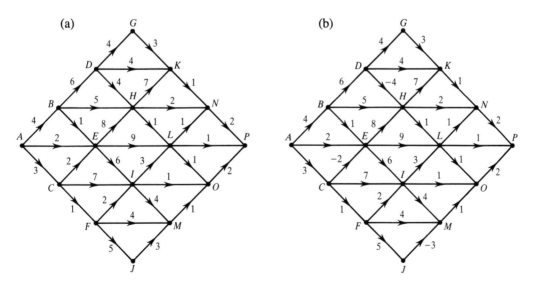

SOLUTIONS

1 Critical path analysis

1.2 Start times

Suppose that the activities in the above network can start at 9 a.m.

(a) What is the earliest possible time for completing the work?

(b) To achieve this earliest possible completion time, what is:

   (i) the earliest possible start time for each activity;

   (ii) the latest possible finishing time for each activity?

(a) 1.30 p.m.

(b)

	(i)	(ii)
A Clear and prepare site	9.00 a.m.	10.00 a.m.
B Set edging	10.00 a.m.	11.30 a.m.
C Lay hardcore for path	11.00 a.m.	12.00 p.m.
D Spread gravel on path	11.30 a.m.	1.00 p.m.
E Dig and fertilise ground	10.00 a.m.	12.00 p.m.
F Plant shrubs	12.00 p.m.	1.00 p.m.
G Tidy site	1.00 p.m.	1.30 p.m.

Exercise 1

1 (a)

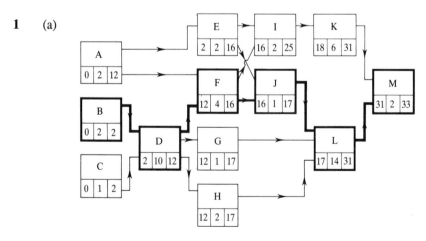

(b) The critical path is shown with bold lines.

(c) Activity E has a float of 12 days.

2 (a) The project is delayed by 2 days. The critical path is unchanged.

(b) The project is delayed by 1 day. The new critical path is BDGLM.

(c) The project can still be completed in 33 days. The critical path is unchanged.

Note that increasing the time of a critical activity increases the total time by the same amount. Increasing the time of a non-critical acitivity will only affect the total time if the increase is greater than the float of the activity.

3 There are various ways that you might have decided to display the two situations. The following are reasonably simple ways of applying network diagrams.

(a)

(b)

4 (a)

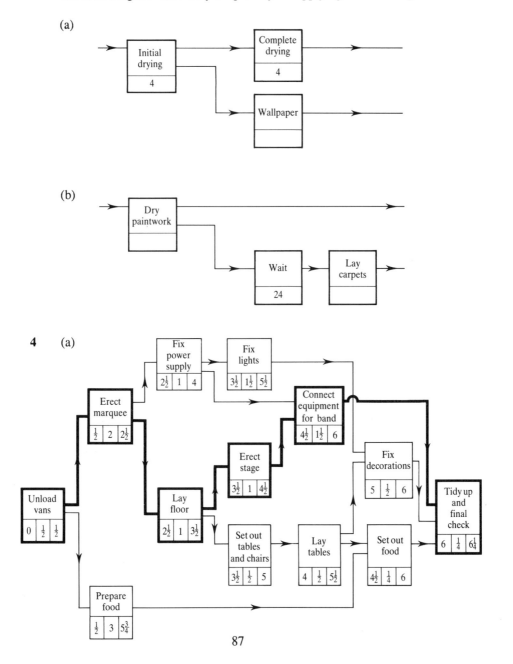

87

(b) $6\frac{1}{4}$ hours are required. The vans must arrive by 12.15 p.m.

(c)

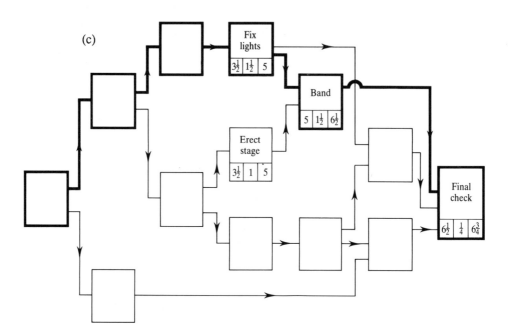

An extra half hour is required. The new critical path is shown with bold lines.

(d)

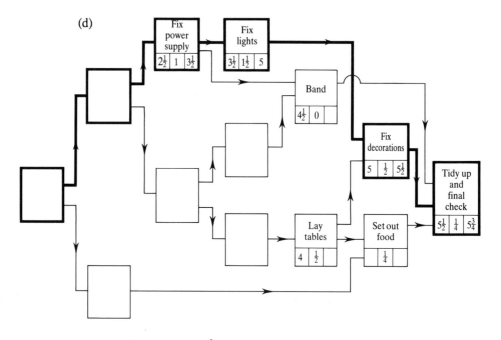

The project takes $5\frac{3}{4}$ hours i.e. half an hour is saved. The new critical path is shown with bold lines.

1.3   Resource levelling

> Draw up a key events plan for the catering team considered in question 4(b) of Exercise 1.

Time when completed	Key events
12.45	Unload vans
2.45	Erect marquee
3.45	Lay floor
4.15	Fix power supply
4.45	Erect stage
5.15	Set out tables & chairs
5.45	Fix lights
5.45	Lay tables
6.00	Prepare food
6.15	Connect equipment for band
6.15	Fix decorations
6.15	Set out food
6.30	Tidy up & final check

> Suggest a way of levelling the labour requirement for this project.

The float available on activities (B) and (C) would suggest reducing the labour allocated to these activities. Assuming that each activity could be done in 3 days by 4 people (instead of in 2 days by 6 people) the resource diagram for labour would be as shown.

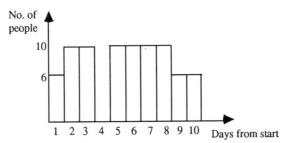

Other ways of changing the plan might have occurred to you. In some circumstances it might be best to simply employ 6 people and take an extra 4 days over the work. In other circumstances it might be better to employ more people on critical activities to bring forward the completion date.

Exercise 2

1   (a)   (i)

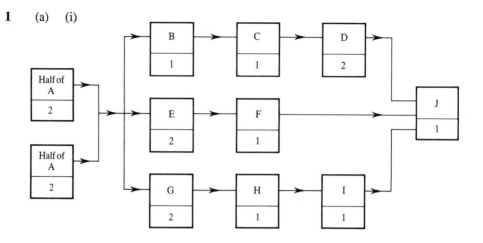

The above is the most likely solution. (I could be done by the person who had done E and F, provided H was finished first.) H could be done before G.

(ii)

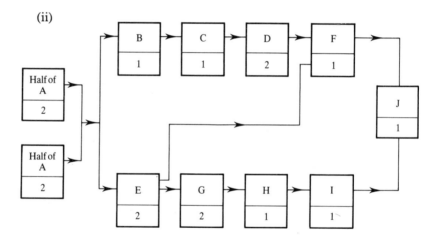

The above is probably the most efficient arrangement.

(b) Gantt chart for (a)(i) ▬▬▬ for (a)(ii) ▬ ▬ ▬ ▬

Activity	Day 1	2	3	4	5	6	7	8	9
A Prepare & fence site (1st person)	▬▬	▬▬							
A Prepare & fence site (2nd person)	▬▬	▬▬							
B Dig pond			▬▬						
C Fill pond, etc.				▬▬					
D Wildlife area					▬▬	▬▬			
E Lay path			▬▬	▬					
F Plant shrubbery					▬▬		▬		
G Lay paved area			▬▬		▬	▬			
H Build rockery					▬▬		▬		
I Plant rockery						▬▬		▬	
J Check & tidy							▬▬		▬

Resources diagrams

(a) (i)

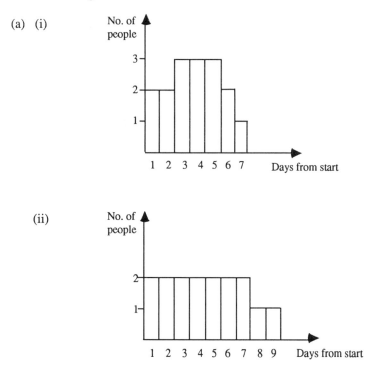

(ii)

2 (a)

Activity		Preceding activities	No. of weeks
A	First meeting	–	–
B	Draft Chapter 1	A	4
C	Draft Chapter 2	A	6
D	Draft Chapter 3	A	6
E	Draft Chapter 4	A	7
F	Draft Chapter 5	A	4
G	Circulate material, etc.	A, B, C, D, E, F	3
H	2nd version Chapter 1	A, B, C, D, E, F, G	3
I	2nd version Chapter 2	A, B, C, D, E, F, G	2
J	2nd version Chapter 3	A, B, C, D, E, F, G	4
K	2nd version Chapter 4	A, B, C, D, E, F, G	3
L	2nd version Chapter 5	A, B, C, D, E, F, G	4
M	Editor's final work	A–L inclusive	5

(b)

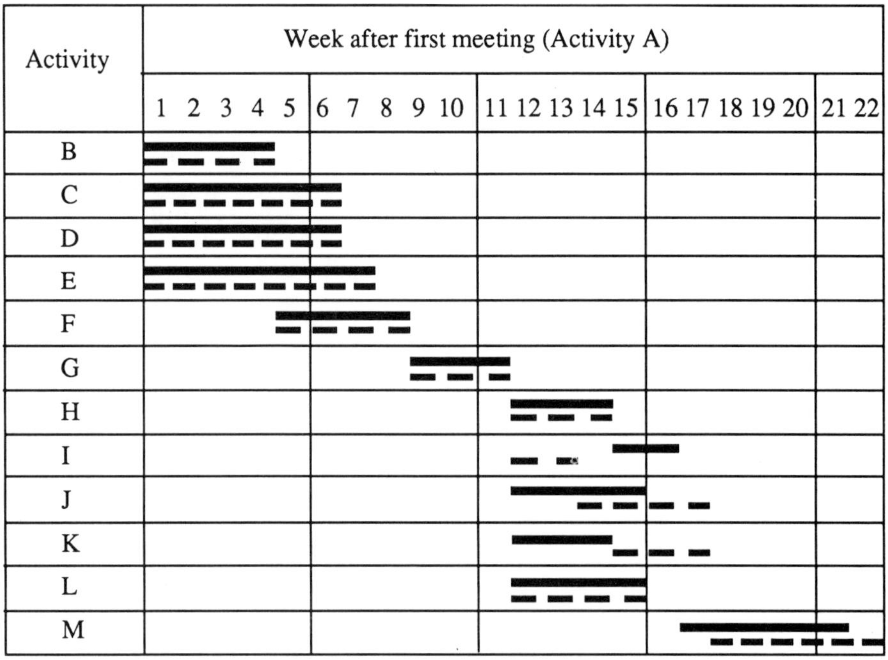

Activity	Week after first meeting (Activity A)				
	1 2 3 4 5	6 7 8 9 10	11 12 13 14 15	16 17 18 19 20	21 22
B	▬▬▬ ▬ ▬ ▬ ▬				
C	▬▬▬▬ ▬ ▬ ▬ ▬ ▬ ▬				
D	▬▬▬ ▬ ▬ ▬ ▬ ▬ ▬				
E	▬▬▬▬ ▬ ▬ ▬ ▬ ▬ ▬ ▬				
F	▬▬▬ ▬ ▬ ▬				
G	▬▬ ▬ ▬ ▬				
H			▬▬ ▬ ▬ ▬		
I			▬ ▬ ▬	▬▬	
J			▬▬▬ ▬ ▬ ▬	▬ ▬	
K			▬▬▬ ▬ ▬ ▬	▬ ▬	
L			▬▬▬ ▬ ▬ ▬ ▬		
M				▬▬▬ ▬ ▬ ▬	▬ ▬

[Chart for (i) is ▬▬▬▬ Chart for (ii) is ▬ ▬ ▬ Slight variations are possible.]

(c)   22 weeks before 30 June, which is 27 January.

(d)

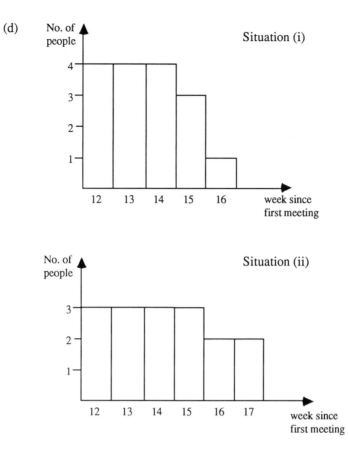

2 Graphs

2.1 The Königsberg bridges

> For each of the drawings below name an eulerian
> trail or a semi-eulerian trail, as appropriate.

(a)   *DECDABCAFE* is one semi-eulerian trail. Any answers will begin at *D* and end
at *E*, or vice versa.

(b)   *ABCADEA* is one eulerian trail. Any answer will begin and end at the same
vertex.

2.2 What is a graph?

> (a)   **Redraw the CPA network given below as a graph
> of vertices and edges only.**
>
> (b)   **How many vertices are there?**
>
> (c)   **How many edges?**

(a)   Replacing each activity by a vertex gives the following underlying graph.

Your graph may **look** very different but should show the same connections between points. You may have chosen to show the order in which the activities
must occur.

Such a directed graph is called a **digraph**.

(b)   10

(c)   9

> **In the graph above, how many different paths are there from *A* to *E*?**

There are 6:

   ABCDE   *ABCFE*   *ACDE*   *ACFE*   *AGCDE*   *AGCFE*

Note that *ACE* is **not** a path because *C* and *E* are not joined by an edge. Also, *AGCBACFE* is **not** a path because *A* and *C* are repeated.

The answer of 6 paths can be obtained easily by noting that there are 3 paths from *A* to *C* and 2 paths from *C* to *E*. Each path from *C* to *E* can be put on the end of each path from *A* to *C* and so there are 3 x 2 = 6 paths from *A* to *E*.

> **Find all the circuits of the graph above.**

ABCA   *ABDA*   *ACDA*   *BCDB*   *ABCDA*   *ABDCA*   *ACBDA*
(*ACDBA* is the same as *ABDCA* and *BCDAB* is the same as *ABCDA*.)

Exercise 1

1   (a)   All vertices must be of even order.

      (b)   Two vertices must be of odd order and all the others even.

2   (a)   There are only two essentially different trees with 4 vertices:

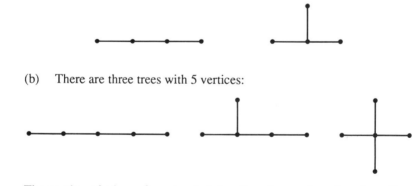

      (b)   There are three trees with 5 vertices:

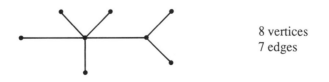

3   The number of edges of any tree is 1 less than the number of vertices. For example:

                                        8 vertices
                                        7 edges

      It is quite difficult to give a rigorous proof of this result.

4   The examples given are as shown:

	Order 4	Order 1
Methane	1	4
Propane	3	8
Isobutane	4	10

Other examples can easily be generated. For example, you could consider a line of n carbon atoms with hydrogen atoms attached as shown.

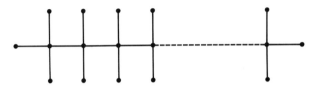

This molecule has n hydrogen atoms at the top and bottom and 1 at each end. The number of vertices of order 1 is therefore $2n + 2$. This can be proved to be generally true and so the chemical formula of the molecules studied by Cayley is $C_n H_{2n+2}$

[N.B. Some textbooks use the term **valency** for the order of a vertex. This corresponds to the use of the word in chemistry.]

5   (a)

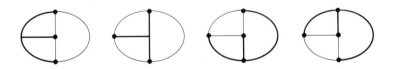

The underlying graph is the same as that of the Wheatstone bridge.

(b)   There are 16 possible spanning trees.

Those with a vertex of order 3:

Others with vertex X of order 1.

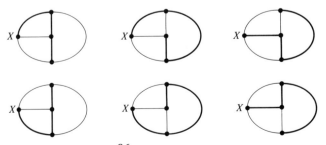

96

Others with vertex X of order 2.

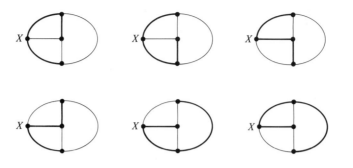

N.B. Because each spanning tree has 4 vertices there are only two essentially

different types of spanning tree, •————•————•————• and ⊥

2.3 Incidence tables

> **(a)** **What is given by the sum of the entries in each row?**
>
> **(b)** **Which other kinds of tables could be used to represent a graph?**

(a) The sum of the entries is the order of the vertex whose name heads the row.

(b) The edges of the graph might be labelled, as shown. Another possibility is to use the regions α, β, γ and δ into which the plane is divided by the edges of the graph.

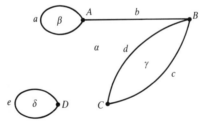

Two possible tables:

	a	b	c	d	e
A	2	1	0	0	0
B	1	0	1	1	0
C	0	0	1	1	0
D	0	0	0	0	2

	a	b	c	d	e
α	1	1	1	1	1
β	1	0	0	0	0
γ	0	0	1	1	0
δ	0	0	0	0	1

> (a) Write out incidence tables for these two graphs.
>
> (b) By rearranging rows and columns show that the graphs are isomorphic.

(a)

	A	B	C	D
A	0	1	1	0
B	1	0	1	1
C	1	1	0	1
D	0	1	1	0

	P	Q	R	S
P	0	1	0	1
Q	1	0	1	1
R	0	1	0	1
S	1	1	1	0

(b) If the headings of the second table are ordered P, Q, S, R instead of P, Q, R, S, the entries become identical to those in the first table. (Try it!)

> (a) Give an alternative correspondence between graphs 1 and 2.
>
> (b) Can the graphs be isomorphic under a correspondence with $A \leftrightarrow Q$?
>
> (c) Which of these properties of a graph are unchanged in an isomorphism?
>
>   - The number of vertices.
>   - The number of edges.
>   - The length of an edge.
>   - The straightness of an edge.

(a) $A \leftrightarrow R, \ B \leftrightarrow S, \ C \leftrightarrow Q, \ D \leftrightarrow P$

You can check that this is an isomorphism by drawing up the table for the second graph with headings in the order R, S, Q, P.

(b)   No, since A has order 2 whilst Q has order 3.

(c)   The numbers of vertices and edges are unchanged. Lengths and shapes of edges may change.

City centre streets are often one-way and then a digraph would be appropriate to indicate the direction of traffic flow. In a DC network the flow of electrons (or opposing conventional current) might be shown in a digraph. The linkages (edges) in a family tree show the flow of time and so a family tree may be regarded as a digraph. In the remaining two examples there is no directional flow so an undirected graph is more appropriate.

(a) What is given by the sum of the entries in each row?

(b) Why is this table not symmetrical about its main diagonal?

(a) The sum of row entries is the number of edges directed away from the vertex whose name heads the row.

(b) Symmetry about the leading diagonal is a feature of tables of **symmetric relations**; in the case of graphs symmetry would require, for example, that if vertex A can be reached from vertex B then vertex B can be reached from vertex A. Such symmetry is not a property of digraphs.

Exercise 2

1
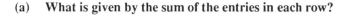

	A	B	C	D
A	0	1	0	2
B	1	0	1	1
C	0	1	0	2
D	2	1	2	0

2
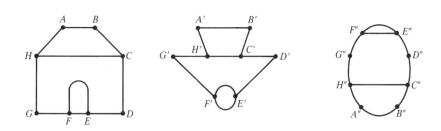

Under the isomorphisms, $A \leftrightarrow A' \leftrightarrow A''$, and so on.

3   (a) and (c) are isomorphic.

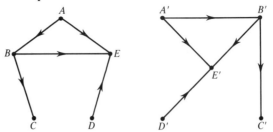

4E   (a)   An explanation can be given by constructing the structure of propane C_3H_8 starting with a C atom and its four edges.

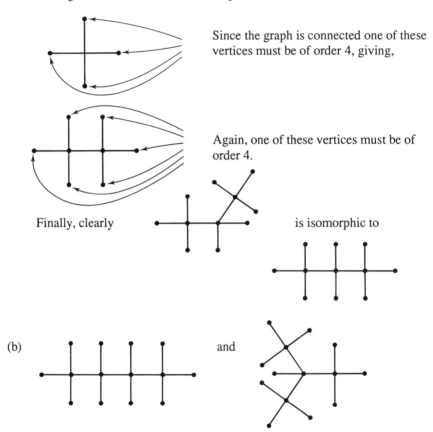

Since the graph is connected one of these vertices must be of order 4, giving,

Again, one of these vertices must be of order 4.

Finally, clearly   is isomorphic to

(b)   and

are not isomorphic because in the second structure (isobutane) a vertex of order 4 is adjacent to three other vertices of order 4 while in the first structure all the vertices of order 4 are adjacent to either one or two vertices of order 4.

(c)   There are three forms of C_5H_{12}, corresponding to these graphs.

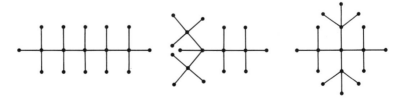

100

2.4   Graphs in practice

> **Write down the orders of the five vertices.**

$o(A) = 0,$ $o(B) = 4,$ $o(C) = 3,$ $o(D) = 4,$ $o(E) = 1$

> **Think of several different networks of practical importance: air routes, oil pipe lines and so on. In each case decide what degree of connectedness is:**
>
> • essential;
> • desirable;
> • undesirable.

Electrical and road networks and CPA diagrams have already been mentioned in the text. There are many other networks of practical importance, including inland waterways, irrigation channels and flow diagrams for arithmetic algorithms.

The question of connectedness is discussed in the text.

Exercise 3

1

	connected	simple	complete
(a)	x	x	x
(b)	✓	x	x
(c)	✓	✓	✓

Graph (c) is K_3.

2   (a) K_4 has 6 edges.

(b) K_n has $\frac{1}{2}n(n-1)$ edges. (Each of the n vertices is joined to $n-1$ other vertices. The product $n(n-1)$ must be halved because each edge has been counted twice.)

3

	A	B	C	D	E	F
A	0	11	0	10	0	9
B	11	0	12	6	0	0
C	0	12	0	14	0	0
D	10	6	14	0	10	0
E	0	0	0	10	0	20
F	9	0	0	0	20	0

2.5   Planar graphs

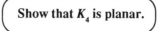

Show that K_4 is planar.

K_4 may be drawn as a plane graph:

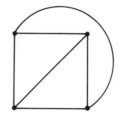

(a)   Verify Euler's formula for the plane graph above.

(b)   Draw K_4 as a plane graph and verify Euler's formula for this graph.

(a)   For the given graph, $v = 6$, $e = 7$, $f = 3$.
       Therefore $v - e + f = 6 - 7 + 3 = 2$

(b)

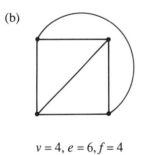

$v = 4$, $e = 6$, $f = 4$

$v - e + f = 4 - 6 + 4 = 2$

3 Spanning trees

3.1 Making connections

> Draw a connecting system which has a smaller total length than either of the two illustrated above.

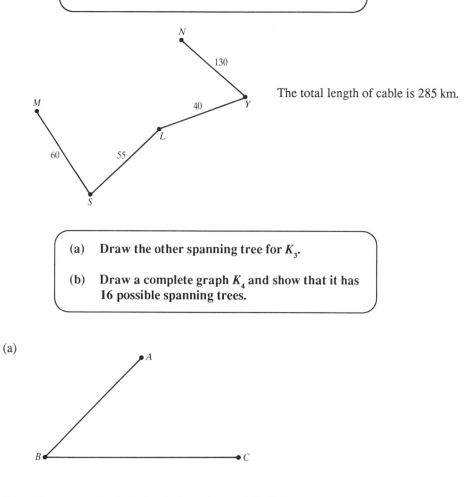

The total length of cable is 285 km.

> (a) Draw the other spanning tree for K_3.
>
> (b) Draw a complete graph K_4 and show that it has 16 possible spanning trees.

(a)

(b) For the graph labelled as below, the possible links to give spanning trees are:

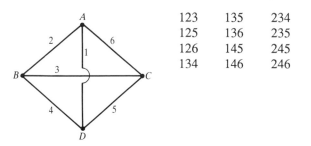

123	135	234	256
125	136	235	346
126	145	245	356
134	146	246	456

3.2   Prim's algorithm

> **Show that by starting at A, you can use Prim's algorithm to give you either the same spanning tree or a different one which also has length 13.**

Same tree

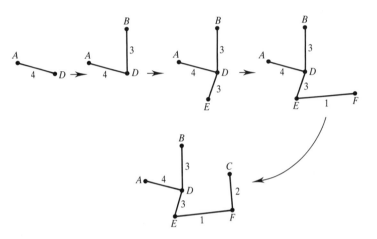

Different tree

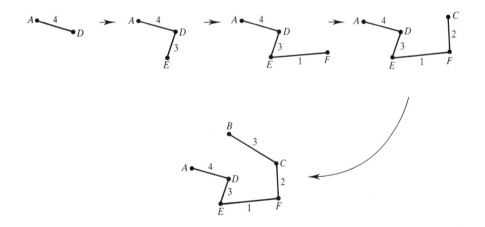

Exercise 1

1   One possible order of joining is:

$A - C$; $C - D$; $C - E$; $D - F$; $F - G$; $F - H$; $A - B$; giving:

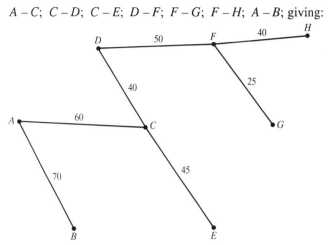

The total length of
pathway is 330 m.

2   One possible sequence is:

Leeds – Sheffield; Sheffield – Manchester; Sheffield – Nottingham;
Nottingham – Leicester; Leicester – Birmingham; Leeds – Liverpool;
Birmingham – Bristol; Bristol – Southampton; Southampton – London.

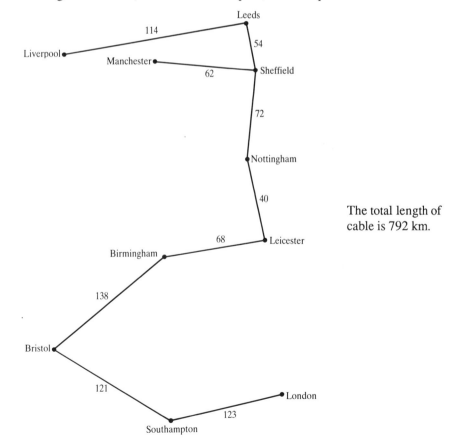

The total length of
cable is 792 km.

3.3 Computing with Prim's algorithm

> **Repeat Example 1 using the procedure of this section.**

The table is:

From\To	A	B	C	D	E	F
A	X	5	X	4	8	X
B	5	X	3	3	X	X
C	X	3	X	7	X	2
D	4	3	7	X	3	X
E	8	X	X	3	X	1
F	X	X	2	X	1	X

A spanning tree of length 13 units should be obtained.

Exercise 2

1 (a) It must represent a complete graph since the only missing links are $A - A, B - B$, and so on.

(b) For example, join: $A - D$; $D - B$; $B - C$ and $D - E$.
                             7   4   5   8

The tree is of length 24 units.

2 For example, join: $C - B$; $B - D$; $B - V$; $V - H$; $V - T$ and $T - G$.
                             350   100   150   100   200   300

The total length of the paths is 1200 m or 1.2 km.

3.4 Kruskal's algorithm

> **Explain clearly how to complete the solution. You should obtain a minimum spanning tree of length 13 units.**

$B - D$ would form a circuit, so join $E - F$ and then $B - E$.

The tree has length 13 units.

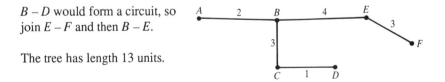

Exercise 3

1 Join: Dunes – Scrape; East – Heath; Scrape – Heath (or Scrape – East);
              12   15   18

   Beach – Dunes; Centre – Tree; Tree – Dunes; Centre – Gravel Pit
        20   23   24   25

The total cost is 137 x £100, or £13 700.

2 £1800 can be saved, since £11 900 is spent by joining:

   Dune – Scrape; East – Heath; Scrape – East (Or Scrape – Heath);
        12   15   18

   Dunes – Beach; Gravel Pit – Centre; Centre – Heath
        20   25   29

4 Shortest paths

4.1 A greedy algorithm

> **Find the shortest path through the graph from A to G.**

ABCDFG 15 days

4.2 Dynamic programming

> (a) **Use the dynamic programming algorithm to find the quickest path from port A to port G.**
>
> (b) **If there are n vertices in a graph, what is the maximum possible number of edges in a path through the graph?**

(a)

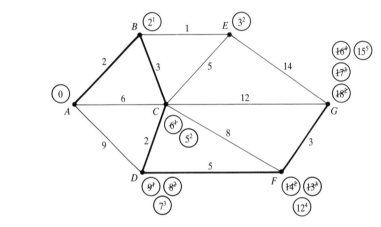

ABCDFG 15 days

(b) When tracing a **path**, no vertex is passed through more than once (see Chapter 2, Section 2.2). Hence for a graph with n vertices the maximum number of stages for a path through the graph is $n - 1$.

Exercise 1

1	*ACBFEG*	£2600
2	*ABCFG*	16 days
3	*ABFG*	41 units
4	*AEHIJ*	15 minutes

4.3 Dijkstra's algorithm

> How can you be sure there is no quicker route to B?

As all the edge weightings are positive any other route to B via C or D must be greater than 2. (In fact, any route via C to B will be greater than 6 and any route via D to B will be greater than 9.)

> (a) Complete the solution using Dijkstra's algorithm.
>
> (b) Which of Dijkstra's algorithm and dynamic programming do you prefer?

(a)

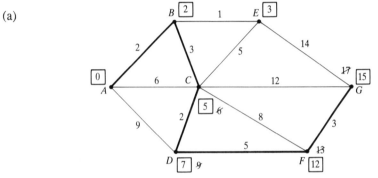

ABCDFG   15 days

Exercise 2

1   (a)   Tours–Poitiers–Angoulême–Bordeaux   328 km

      (b)   Tours–Châteauroux–Limoges–Périgueux   296 km

2   *ABEFHJ*   22 minutes.

3   An explanation on how to use this table is given on the following page.

From\To	T	S	Po	C	A	L	Pé	B
Tours	[0]	[61]	[104]	[70]				
	–	61	104	70	–	–	–	–
Saumur	6̶1̶	–	9̶2̶ 153	–	2̶0̶0̶ 261	–	–	–
Poitiers	1̶0̶4̶	9̶2̶	–	120	110 [214]	–	[195]	–
Châteauroux	7̶0̶	–	1̶2̶0̶ 190	–	–	125	–	–
Angoulême	–	2̶0̶0̶	1̶1̶0̶	–	–	103	8̶5̶ 299	114 [328]
Limoges	–	–	–	1̶2̶5̶	1̶0̶3̶ 298	–	101 [296]	–
Périgueux	–	–	–	–	8̶5̶	1̶0̶1̶	–	1̶2̶0̶ 416
Bordeaux	–	–	–	–	1̶1̶4̶	–	1̶2̶0̶	–

109

As you move through the table, keep a running total of distances from Tours. Label Tours to Tours zero, box it and cross out all other values in the Tours column. Look at the first row (Tours to Saumur, Poitiers and Châteauroux) and box the shortest distance (Tours to Saumur). There is no shorter route to Saumur and so all other values **to** Saumur can be deleted (Poitiers to Saumur and Angoulême to Saumur). Now investigate all direct routes from Saumur (Saumur to Poitiers and Angoulême) and fill in the total distance of Poitiers and Angoulême from Tours. Box the shortest running total from Tours (Tours to Châteauroux). There is no shorter route to Châteauroux so all other routes to Châteauroux can be deleted (Poitiers to Châteauroux and Limoges to Châteauroux). Move through the table in this fashion until you find the shortest (boxed) distance from Tours to Bordeaux. Check that each column of the table has, at most, one boxed value – the shortest distance from Tours to that town.

4.4 Choosing an algorithm

> (a) Use both algorithms to find the shortest path through the above graph from A to Y.
>
> (b) Explain why Dijkstra's algorithm is usually more efficient than dynamic programming in finding the shortest path through a graph.

(a)   *ABEHLQTWY*   14 units

(b)   Dynamic programming systematically investigates 1-stage routes, 2-stage routes and so on, until the optimum path has been found to **each** vertex on the graph.

Dijkstra's algorithm is more efficient in that it does not necessarily investigate each vertex in finding the shortest path from start to finish vertices. For example, for this particular problem, vertices K, O, R, S, V and X have not been approached in finding the shortest path from A to Y and shortest paths from A to $G, J, K, M, N, O, R, S, U, V$ and X have not been investigated.

Exercise 3

1   (a)   If the delivery service does not deliver along the section C–D, it will incur extra costs in making special trips to the company's warehouse to pick up the next batch of parcels. Being able to make a pick-up while delivering parcels is therefore a bonus for the delivery service and can be represented, using a negative weighting, as a saving rather than a cost.

    (b)

B: ACB	£8		*E: ACBE*	£13
C: AC	£6		*F: ACDF*	£2
D: ACD	£1		*G: ACDFG*	£15

2   (a)   *ADECHI*   16 units   (b)   *ADCBGI*   27 units

3   St. Louis–Indianapolis–Columbus–Washington   811 miles

4   *ACBDHILNO*   77 weeks

5 Line inspection

5.1 The Chinese postman problem

> **What do you think is the shortest route, starting from *A*?**

In answering this question you will realise that some streets will have to be retraced and that in the optimal case the street-length retraced will be least. The text follows up this idea.

> (a) **Find an Eulerian trail, starting at *A*.**
>
> (b) **Could you start at *any* point in the graph?**
>
> (c) **What is the total length of the optimal route?**

(a) *ABCDECFEFAFBA* is one possible trail.

(b) Yes. The starting point in a trail is arbitrary. For example, the trail in (a) is the same as *DECFEFAFBABCD*.

(c) The total length is the sum of all edge-lengths together with the lengths of those repeated, that is 63 + 14 = 77 (770 metres).

> **Think of three other kinds of network requiring such inspections.**

Examples include road networks (examined for surface wear or treated with grit in frosty weather, for example); and the various networks under city streets – sewers, gas pipes, electrical and water supply lines.

Exercise 1

1   *A* and *D* are the only odd vertices. Streets to be retraced between *A* and *D* have minimum total length 210 m (*AG* + *GE* + *ED* or *AG* + *GF* + *FE* + *ED*). To this must be added the sum of all the street lengths, 1110 m. So the optimal route has length 1320 m.

2   The odd vertices are A, C, D and E. These may be paired off as:
          $A–C, D–E$, or $A–D, C–E$ or $A–E, C–D$.

Shortest distances:

$AC = 10$, $DE = 9$
$AD = 10$, $CE = 14$
$AE = 7$, $CD = 16$

The best pairing is $A–C, D–E$ giving a total length $74 + 19 = 93$.

5.2   The travelling salesperson's problem

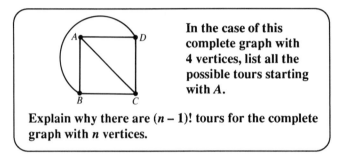

In the case of this complete graph with 4 vertices, list all the possible tours starting with A.

Explain why there are $(n – 1)!$ tours for the complete graph with n vertices.

$ABCDA$, $ABDCA$, $ACBDA$, $ACDBA$, $ADBCA$, $ADCBA$ (6 tours in all)

For the complete graph with n vertices, the vertices may be arranged in $n!$ ways. Any tour can be represented in n ways (for example, the tour $ABCDA$ above may also be represented by $BCDAB$ or $CDABC$ or $DABCD$). Hence the total of distinct tours is $n! \div n = (n – 1)!$

How long would it take a computer performing 100 000 additions each second to make 20! additions?

$20! = 2.43 \times 10^{18}$, so the computer would take 2.43×10^{13} seconds $= 771\ 000$ years (to the nearest thousand years!).

5.3   The nearest neighbour algorithm

Describe what happens if she continues to apply the 'nearest neighbour' algorithm. Modify the algorithm to plan what you consider a reasonable tour.

Columbia – Florence – Charlotte – Salem – Greensboro – Sanford – Raleigh (Asheville is never visited).

Your modification must ensure that all the cities are visited. A suggestion follows in the text.

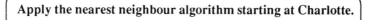

Apply the nearest neighbour algorithm starting at Charlotte.

The algorithm gives the tour:

Charlotte – Salem – Greensboro – Sanford – Raleigh – Florence – Columbia – Asheville – Charlotte

$$78 + 40 + 60 + 42 + 147 + 82 + 153 + 112$$

The total distance is 714 miles.

Exercise 2

1   Salem gives the least mileage (713 miles), closely followed by Asheville and Charlotte (both 714 miles).

2   The routes are:

AECBDA	(length 31)
BCEADB	(as above, in reverse)
CBEADC	(length 31)
DCBEAD	(as above)
ECBADE	(length 33)

You can check (by trying the remaining 19 routes) that 31 is the shortest length possible.

3   AEDCFBA is a route, of length 52, that he might choose. A better route is AFBDCEA of length 41 (found by using the nearest neighbour algorithm starting at B).

5.4   Heuristic methods

Which pairs of edges are cut in the second and third steps?

Second step : AB and FH are cut.
Third step: FG and HA are cut.

5.5   Upper and lower bounds

Exercise 3

1   (a)

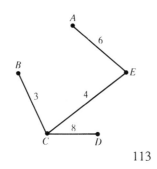

The minimum connector is shown.
An upper bound is:
$$2 \times (3 + 4 + 6 + 8) = 42$$

113

(b) If A is deleted the minimum connector for the remaining vertices is as shown. To $(3 + 4 + 8)$ must be added the lengths of the shortest edges from A, giving a total of $(3 + 4 + 8) + (6 + 7) = 28$.

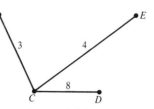

Other lower bounds, found by deleting B, C, D and E are 26, 27, 30 and 27 respectively. The best estimate to the optimal tour is the greatest of these, 30.

2 The minimum spanning tree is constructed from the table as follows: B–D, D–A, A–E, E–F, F–C. Its edges total $3 + 5 + 4 + 4 + 5 = 21$. Using the MST method an upper bound is $2 \times 21 = 42$.

Using the prescribed method lower bounds are as follows:

deleting A : $4 + 5 + 6 + 3 + 4 + 5 = 27$
deleting B : $4 + 5 + 4 + 6 + 3 + 7 = 29$
deleting C : $3 + 5 + 4 + 4 + 5 + 6 = 27$
deleting D : $4 + 4 + 5 + 7 + 3 + 5 = 28$
deleting E : $3 + 5 + 6 + 5 + 4 + 4 = 27$
deleting F : $3 + 5 + 6 + 4 + 4 + 5 = 27$

The greatest of the lower bounds is 29.

3E The procedure yields lower bounds for TSP tour lengths. If it gives a tour then there can be no tour of shorter length. (The procedure has given a greatest lower bound.) So the condition is sufficient. On the other hand, the procedure will not yield a tour in general, so the condition is not necessary.

5.6 Scheduling

(a) Sketch a network to illustrate the information.

(b) Use the nearest neighbour algorithm starting from A to find one possible cycle which might provide an acceptable solution.

(c) Copy the table of values and ring the items you chose, commenting on the pattern formed by the rings.

(a)

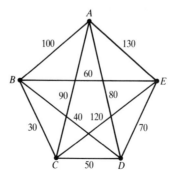

114

(b) *ADBCEA* is the cycle found using the suggested method.

(c)

	A	B	C	D	E
A	–	100	90	(80)	130
B	100	–	(30)	40	60
C	90	30	–	50	(120)
D	80	(40)	50	–	70
E	(130)	60	120	70	–

Every row and every column contains exactly one ringed entry.

> **Restricting your choice of items to one from each row and column is a necessary condition for the formation of a tour but not sufficient.**
>
> **Why would this pattern of rings be unsatisfactory?**
>
> | | A | B | C | D | E |
> |---|---|---|---|---|---|
> | A | | O | | | |
> | B | | | O | | |
> | C | O | | | | |
> | D | | | | | O |
> | E | | | | O | |

The table may be partitioned like this.

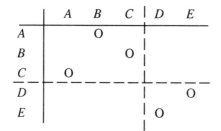

You will see that there are two 'sub-cycles' *ABCA* and *DED*, so that whichever first step is chosen a complete cycle can never be made.

> **Make a copy of the table and adjust the values for rows B, C, D and E in a similar way.**

From\To	A	B	C	D	E	Minimum
		20	10	0	50	
A	–	~~100~~	~~90~~	~~80~~	~~130~~	80
	70		0	10	30	
B	~~100~~	–	~~30~~	~~40~~	~~60~~	30
	60	0		20	90	
C	~~90~~	~~30~~	–	~~50~~	~~120~~	30
	40	0	10		30	
D	~~80~~	~~40~~	~~50~~	–	~~70~~	40
	70	0	60	10		
E	~~130~~	~~60~~	~~120~~	~~70~~	–	60

(a) For example, if the decision is made to include *CB*, *BE* and *AD*, which are all zero in the reduced table, what other choices must be made for the two remaining items?

(b) What is the overall total in this case?

(c) Is this better than totals you can find using the nearest neighbour method with different starting points?

(d) You may like to try some other combinations of zero items.

(a) *D–C* and *E–A* $(10 + 30)$

(b) The result is a cycle *ADCBEA* of time 350 minutes.

(c) Using the nearest neighbour algorithm these results are obtained.

$$B - C - D - E - A - B$$
$$30 + 50 + 70 + 130 + 100 \quad = 380$$

$$C - B - D - E - A - C$$
$$30 + 40 + 70 + 130 + 90 \quad = 360$$

$$D - B - C - A - E - D$$
$$50 + 30 + 90 + 130 + 70 \quad = 370$$

$$E - B - C - D - A - E$$
$$60 + 30 + 50 + 80 + 130 \quad = 350$$

The last cycle is the same as *ADCBEA*, but in reverse. No improvement has been made using the nearest neighbour algorithm.

Exercise 4

1 (a) The cycle of Red – Black – Blue – Green –Yellow – White – Red gives a time of 115 minutes. When the nearest neighbour algorithm is applied with other starting colours, the time given is greater than 2 hours (times range from 124 to 140 minutes).

(b) 'Row-reduced' matrix:

						Row min.
–	15	5	0	10	5	25
0	–	5	5	10	25	10
0	25	–	10	15	14	10
0	20	10	–	20	5	10
0	15	2	10	–	10	10
0	20	14	5	15	–	10

'Column-reduced' matrix:

–	0	3	0	0	0
0	–	3	5	0	20
0	10	–	10	5	9
0	5	8	–	10	0
0	0	0	10	–	5
0	5	12	5	5	–
Column min. 0	15	2	0	10	5

As you have seen, Σ row minima + Σ column minima is a lower bound for the cycle. In this case $75 + 32 = 107$ minutes is a lower bound; the foreman's suggestion is unattainable.

Miscellaneous exercise

1 (a)

Event	Preceding events
A	–
B	A
C	B
D	–
E	D
F	E
G	D
H	G
I	H
J	C, F, I
K	J

(Events E and F could be in the reverse order, but it does not seem very practical to carry them both out at the same time.)

(b)

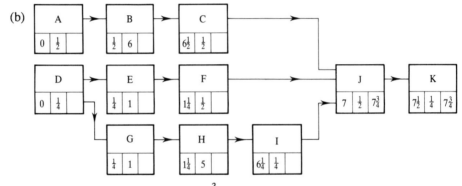

The minimum complete time is $7\frac{3}{4}$ hours, so they must start work by 9.15 a.m.

2 (a) The number of edges of a spanning tree is always one less than the number of vertices i.e. $n - 1$.

(b) (i) $3 + 3 + 3 + 4 + 4 = 17$

(ii) The edges of lengths 3 and 4 might contain a circuit. (An equivalent answer is to say that these 5 edges might not span all the vertices of the graph.)

(iii) The only way to obtain 19 from the given lengths is $3 + 3 + 4 + 4 + 5$.

The required graph must therefore be built up from a tree with edges of lengths 3, 3, 4, 4 and 5. Furthermore, the three edges of length 3 must form a circuit so that not all of them can be kept in a spanning tree. An example is:

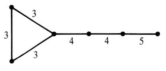

The edges of lengths 7, 7 and 8 can join any pairs of vertices.

118

3   First suppose the central edge is in the tree:

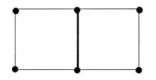

There are 3 ways of choosing two of the left-hand edges and 3 ways of choosing two of the right-hand edges. Thus there are 3 x 3 = 9 trees.

Next suppose the central edge is not in the tree.

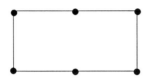

There are 6 ways of discarding one further edge.

The total number of trees is 9 + 6 = 15.

4   (a)   *ADEFJKPQ*: 18 minutes

       (b)   *ABCHLQ* is now one way of obtaining the quickest route of 20 minutes. (There are others!)

5   (a)   (b)

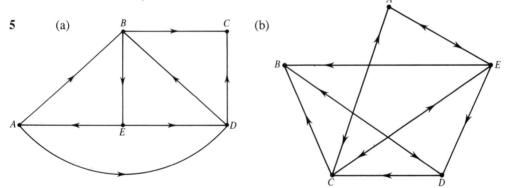

6   *ACDE*: 8 units

Dijkstra's algorithm assumes that once a label representing the 'distance' to a vertex, has been boxed, then there is no possibility of a path with more stages being an improvement. This is true if all the weightings are positive but not if negative weightings are included e.g. Dijkstra's algorithm would box vertex *D* with a permanent value of 4 reached by a one-stage path from A, but the two-stage path *ACD* is an improvement!

7   *ADEG* gives a profit of £780.

8   Manchester–Sheffield–Nottingham–London: 320 km

9   (a)

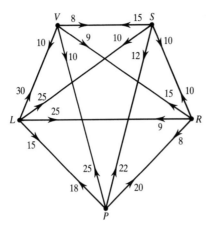

(b)   Nearest neighbour, from V for example, gives:

$$V \xrightarrow{8} S \xrightarrow{10} L \xrightarrow{15} P \xrightarrow{20} R \xrightarrow{15} V \qquad \text{Total 68 minutes}$$

In fact, the optimal solution is:

$$L \xrightarrow{15} P \xrightarrow{25} V \xrightarrow{8} S \xrightarrow{10} R \xrightarrow{9} L \qquad \text{Total 67 minutes}$$

10   Euler's formula can be applied to the n parts separately, taking care to include the infinite face once only. The results are then added to give the generalised formula:

$$v - e + f = 2n - (n-1) = n + 1$$

11   *ADLMN* : 23 hours

12   The minimal spanning tree must have 12 edges. Since it is possible to span the vertices with 12 of the shorter edges (of length 1), this give a minimum length of 12.

For example,

13   (a)

(b)   A similar construction can be used to show that $K_{2,n}$ is planar for any positive integer n.

14 (a, b)

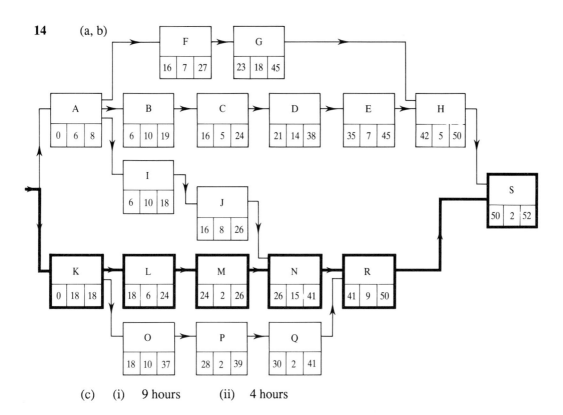

(c) (i) 9 hours (ii) 4 hours

(d) The easiest solution is to have the worker who carries out stages I and J then going on to O, P and Q.

This gives the Gantt chart shown, assuming that each activity is carried out at the earliest possible time. Slight variations are, of course, possible.

Hours from start

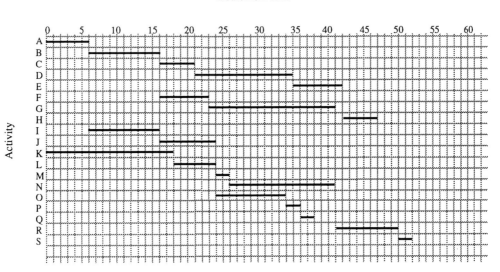

(e)

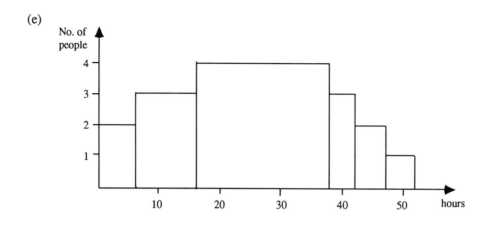

15   (a)   No. There are 2 **odd** vertices.

(b)   Repeat section *AD* to give a total of 82 + 7 = 89 km. One possible route would be *ACGFHEFCBEDBADA,* but there are many others.

(c)

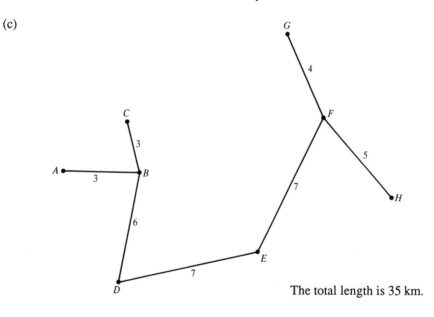

The total length is 35 km.

(d)   Upper bound = 70 km. A much shorter tour can easily be found.

16   (a)   *ACFIOP*: 9 units   (b)   *ABDHLP*: 8 units.

122

COMMENTARIES

1 Critical path analysis

1.1 Scheduling activities

> (a) Subdivide the task of making the sponge sandwich into a set of activities.
>
> (b) Decide on suitable times for each activity.
>
> (c) Draw a network for the task and hence estimate the least time required to make a sponge sandwich.
>
> (d) How many people are needed if the sponge is to be made in the least possible time?

(a),(b) Possible activities and times are as shown in the diagram below.

(c)

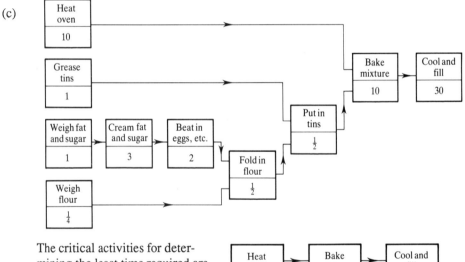

The critical activities for determining the least time required are as shown. These give a total time of 50 minutes.

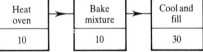

In this simple example, one obvious conclusion from the network would be one well known to experienced cooks:

You should preheat the oven **before** starting the other activities.

(d) Only one person is needed. This person should start by turning the oven on and can then do all the other activities which are needed to prepare the mixture for baking. In general, you should ignore the availability of workers and resources when determining the critical path. Later, the network diagram can be used to help you determine what resources of labour and material will be required at each stage.

Manufacturing barbecues

1   As the paint takes 16 hours to dry, the bolting and packaging must be done on barbecues painted the previous day.

There are several possible solutions. In the one shown below, they each work on and complete their own barbecues. There are solutions, where, for example, one does the welding on all 6 barbecues and the other does all the painting and so it is possible to cater for specialist skills.

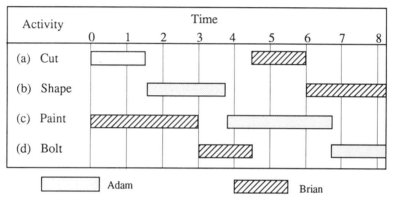

Note that in this solution Brian paints barbecues which he shaped the previous day.

2   The machinery for cutting is only being used for 3 hours and so is available for 5 hours which is enough time to cut sheet metal for 10 barbecues.

The machinery for shaping and welding is free for $3\frac{3}{4}$ hours which is enough time to shape and weld 5 barbecues.

The machinery needed for finishing and painting is already being used for 6 hours and so is only available for $2\frac{1}{4}$ hours. This is sufficient time to finish and paint just 2 barbecues.

An extra person would enable them to produce just 2 extra barbecues per day because of the restriction on the time needed to finish and paint. There are various options:

-     employ someone part time for $5\frac{1}{2}$ hours to produce 2 barbecues per day;
-     employ someone full time and stagger the working day by $\frac{3}{4}$ hour so that 3 hours become available for finishing and painting;
-     invest in more machinery for finishing and painting and produce 3 extra barbecues in the normal working day.

Notice that there is no time to set aside for administrative work. It might be sensible to employ someone full time even though only 2 extra barbecues are produced. Such a person could relieve either Adam or Brian during the day to give them time for administration.

2 Graphs

2.1 The Königsberg bridges

> (a) Show that the line drawing accurately represents the way in which land masses are connected by bridges.
>
> (b) Count the number of edges at each vertex.
>
> (c) Hence explain why the seven bridges walk is impossible.

(a) It may be helpful to ring the letters A, B, C, D and join them across the bridges, as shown.

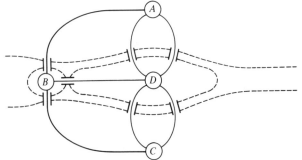

(b) Three edges meet at A, B and C, five at D.

(c) For any vertex in the seven bridges walk, for every entry to the vertex there must be a corresponding exit, therefore the vertex must have an even number of edges. Since the walk is to finish where it started, this argument applies even to the starting vertex.

Extension

If the walk does not need to end where it started then there must be one more exit from the starting vertex than there are entries i.e. the vertex has an odd number of edges. The finishing vertex must have one more entry than exits and so is also odd.

Therefore all the vertices need to be even if the walk is to end where it started. If there are exactly two odd vertices the walk is possible if it starts at one of the odd vertices and finishes at the other.

Traversability

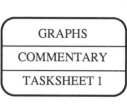
1 From the figure given it can be seen that traversability is possible from one vertex. By symmetry it is possible from any other vertex.

2

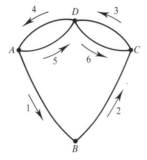

A trace starting from *B* must first visit *A* or *C*. If it visits *A*, the only traces which do not repeat edges are *BADA*, *BADCB* and *BADCDA*. None of these includes all the edges. There is a similar argument by symmetry for traces starting *BC*.

Traces from *A* finish at a different vertex, *C*. Traces in question 1 all start and finish at the same vertex.

3

     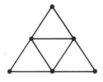

Not traversable   Traversable from any vertex   Traversable from *X* and *Y* only

[category (c)]   [category (a)]   [category (b)]

4 When all the vertices are even the drawing is in category (a); when there are exactly two odd vertices it is in category (b); otherwise it is in category (c).

The Königsberg bridge drawing has four odd vertices and so falls into category (c).

K_5 *is non-planar*

1 Faces with one edge are in loops. Faces with two edges are between multiple connections.

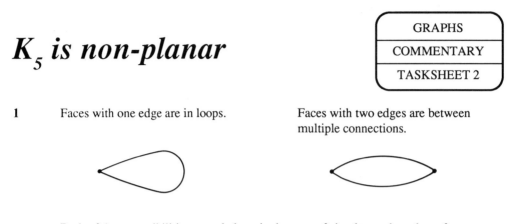

Both of these possibilities are ruled out in the case of simple graphs, whose faces must therefore have at least three edges.

2

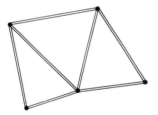

Every edge belongs to two faces and so is included twice when the boundary edges of all the faces are counted face by face. You may like to think in terms of 'half-edges', each 'half-edge' having half the thickness of an edge.

Since for each face there are at least 3 'half-edges', for f faces there are at least $3f$ 'half-edges'. If there are e edges then there are $2e$ 'half-edges' and this number must be at least equal to $3f$. In fact, the only case where $3f = 2e$ is in K_3.

3 (a) For K_5, $v = 5$ and $e = 10$.

(b) If K_5 were drawn in plane form, by Euler's formula: $f = e - v + 2 = 7$

4 Then $3f = 21$, $2e = 20$, so $3f > 2e$, contrary to the results in question 2. Hence the assumption that K_5 can be drawn in plane form is false; that is K_5 is not planar.

5 The most obvious extension is that K_n is non-planar for $n \geq 5$. You should find this more general result quite easy to prove (see Exercise 3, question 2).

6E In a bipartite graph the vertices fall into two disjoint sets (here $\{A, B, C\}$ and $\{W, E, G\}$), edges joining members of one set to members of the other with no direct connections between members of the same set. This should help you to explain why for any bipartite graph $4f \leq 2e$.

If the utilities graph were drawn in plane form, $f = e - v + 2 = 5$. Then $4f = 20$, $2e = 18$ and so $4f > 2e$. As in the case of K_5 this contradition of the formula $4f \leq 2e$ means that the graph $K_{3,3}$ is not planar.

3 Spanning trees

3.1 Making connections

> (a) **Draw a possible spanning tree for the points A to F and write down its length.**
>
> (b) **Try to find a minimum spanning tree and write down its length. Discuss with other students the method you used to do it.**
>
> (c) **Write down a series of rules which you think gives a minimum spanning tree and check that it works for a different set of points and distances.**

(a) Any spanning tree you may have drawn will have 5 edges. The one shown below has total length $6 + 3 + 2 + 2 + 3 = 16$.

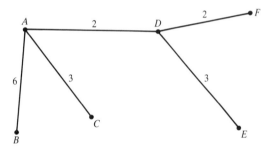

(b) The minimum spanning tree has length $1 + 2 + 3 + 2 + 2 = 10$.

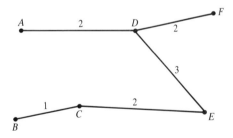

(c) For small graphs it is reasonably easy to 'spot' minimum (or nearly minimum) spanning trees. The work of this chapter is aimed at investigating sets of rules which will **always** lead to the minimum spanning tree, irrespective of how complicated the original graph is.

Kruskal's algorithm

1 The following procedure can be used.

Circle the least element in the table. (If there is more than one choice, pick one at random.) Use indices to indicate that the joined points are now in the same set.

From\To	A	B¹	C	D¹	E
A		10	8	7	10
B			5	④	9
C				7	10
D					8
E					

Repeatedly circle the smallest element which does not join two points already in the same set. Indicate that the newly joined points are now in the same set. (This labelling of points ensures that cycles cannot be formed.)

After several repetitions, Table 2 looks like this.

From\To	A¹	B¹	C¹	D¹	E¹
A		10	8	⑦	10
B			⑤	④	9
C				7	10
D					⑧
E					

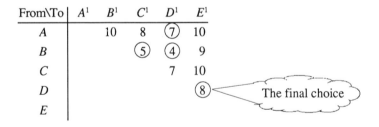

The solution is

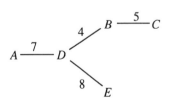

(continued)

130

2 After 2 steps, the table is as shown.

From\To	B	C	D¹	E²	G	H²	S¹	T
B		X	20	X	30	X	X	24
C			X	X	25	29	31	23
D				22	X	X	(12)	24
E					X	(15)	18	X
G						X	X	X
H							18	X
S								X
T								

E and *H* are in set 2 as they are not linked to either *D* or *S*.

The next stage could be:

From\To	B	C	D¹	E¹	G	H¹	S¹	T
B		X	20	X	30	X	X	24
C			X	X	25	29	31	23
D				22	X	X	(12)	24
E					X	(15)	(18)	X
G						X	X	X
H							18	X
S								X
T								

Both *E* and *H* can now go in to set 1 as the **new** link *E–S* links set 2 to set 1.

One possibility for the complete table is then:

From\To	B¹	C¹	D¹	E¹	G¹	H¹	S¹	T¹
B		X	(20)	X	30	X	X	24
C			X	X	(25)	29	31	(23)
D				22	X	X	(12)	(24)
E					X	(15)	(18)	X
G						X	X	X
H							18	X
S								X
T								

The minimum spanning tree has length 137 as before.

3 Solutions can often be found quickly using Kruskal's algorithm 'by hand'. However, programming a computer to avoid producing cycles introduces complexities which are not necessary in the case of Prim's algorithm.

Furthermore, Prim's algorithm requires fewer elements to be checked for minimality at each stage.

4 Shortest paths

4.1 A greedy algorithm

> (a) For the graph above, trace a path from *A* to *G*, leaving each vertex by the edge with least weight. Does this 'greedy' algorithm give you the shortest path through the graph?
>
> (b) Try to develop an algorithm that will give the shortest path. Try the algorithm out on a fellow student. Does it work?

(a) This 'greedy' method traces the path *ABECDFG*.

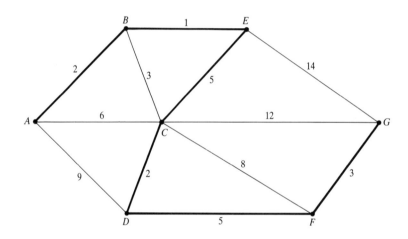

The new path takes 18 days, whereas you have already seen that there is a path which takes only 15 days.

This straightforward 'greedy' algorithm cannot be relied upon to give the shortest path through a graph.

(b) There are many possible ideas you might have tried. If your method does always seem to work you might like to discuss it with your teacher. It will also be interesting to compare it with the methods given later in this chapter.

Longest paths and negative weightings

1 (a) Dynamic programming builds up a set of optimum paths involving first 1-stage routes, then 2-stage routes and so on, **always leaving open the possibility that a path with more stages might be an improvement**. In effect the 'length' of the path to each vertex is continually updated and so the algorithm can cope with 'longer' paths resulting from the inclusion of additional stages (edges).

Longest path: *ADCFGH*   19 units

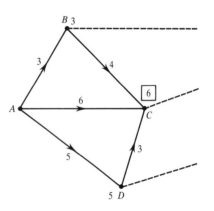

Dijkstra's algorithm does not, in effect, have a 'built-in memory' and so once a value has been boxed, the algorithm does not allow for it to be improved. For example, adapting the algorithm and boxing the **largest** value, vertex *C* takes the permanent value 6 which is obviously not the longest path from *A* to *C*. Adapting Dijkstra's algorithm for longest paths does not seem to work.

(b) Each edge represents an activity and the value on each edge represents the time required to carry out the activity. The network indicates the dependencies between the activities, for example, activity *C* to *F* must take place after completion of activities *B* to *C*, *A* to *C* and *D* to *C*.

For completion of the 'project' all the individual activities must be completed and so the shortest possible finish date will depend upon the start date and the **critical path** – the longest path through the network – assuming necessary resources are available.

The critical path for this network, from *A* to *H*, is 19 units of time and so the shortest period in which the project could be completed is 19 units of time.

2 (a) The optimum path in this case will be the path which reduces costs to a minimum. Hence you require the shortest path through the graph from *A* to *G*.

ABCFG   £140

(b) Once a vertex has been boxed, any further route to the boxed vertex will incur an additional weighting. If the weighting is positive this 'permanent' label cannot be reduced. However, if the additional weighting is negative the 'permanent' label may be reduced and hence Dijkstra's algorithm breaks down.

Operations

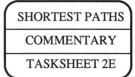

1   A path of 5 edges (or stages)

2   (a)   5 (The new value to each vertex is compared with the present value, zero.)

      (b)   4

      (c)   4 (The vertices with permanent labels need no longer be considered.)

      (d)

Length of path	Number of vertices to consider	Number of additions	Number of comparisons
1	5	5	5 + 4
2	4	4	4 + 3
3	3	3	3 + 2
4	2	2	2 + 1
5	1	1	1
		15	15 + 10

35 operations

      (e)   (i) $1 + 2 + 3 + \ldots + (n-1) = \frac{1 + (n-1)}{2} \times (n-1) = \frac{1}{2} n (n-1)$

            (ii) $\frac{1}{2} n (n-1) + \frac{1 + (n-2)}{2} \times (n-2) = \frac{1}{2} n (n-1) + \frac{1}{2} (n-1) (n-2)$

$$= \frac{1}{2} (n-1) (n + n - 2)$$

$$= (n-1)^2$$

            (iii)   Total = (i) + (ii) $= \frac{1}{2} n (n-1) + (n-1)^2$

$$= \frac{1}{2} n^2 - \frac{1}{2} n + n^2 - 2n + 1$$

$$= \frac{3}{2} n^2 - \frac{5}{2} n + 1$$

3   (a)   The vertices are not compared at this stage as they may be updated if a shorter route is found.

      (b)   4

      (c)   5 additions and 4 comparisons

      (d)   25 additions and 20 comparisons

(continued)

(e)

Length of path	Number of vertices to consider	Number of additions	Number of comparisons
1 or less	6	5	0
2 or less	6	5 x 5	4 x 5
3 or less	6	5 x 5	4 x 5
4 or less	6	5 x 5	4 x 5
5 or less	6	5 x 5	4 x 5
		105	80

A total of 185 operations

(f) (i) $(n - 1) + (n - 1)^2 \times (n - 2) = n^3 - 4n^2 + 6n - 3$

(ii) $(n - 2) \times (n - 1) \times (n - 2) = n^3 - 5n^2 + 8n - 4$

(iii) Total = (i) + (ii) $= 2n^3 - 9n^2 + 14n - 7$

4

n	Dijkstra's algorithm	Dynamic programming
3	7	8
6	40	185
10	126	1233
20	551	12673
100	14751	1911393

(a) Although dynamic programming has wider applications, Dijkstra's algorithm is far more efficient for problems on a realistic scale.

(b) Dynamic programming : $2n^3 - 9n^2 + 14n - 7$ a polynomial of order 3

Dijkstra's algorithm   : $1.5n^2 - 2.5n + 1$ a polynomial of order 2

For large n, n^3 becomes the dominant term for dymamic programming and increases much more rapidly than n^2, the dominant term in Dijkstra's algorithm.

5   Line inspection

5.1   The Chinese postman problem

The handshake lemma

The vertices A, B, C, D represent people. The edges represent handshakes at a gathering.

(a)   What peculiarity of behaviour is exhibited by
      (i) B and C, (ii) D?

(b)   Show that the sum of all the orders of the vertices is even and explain why, in terms of handshakes.

The general rule that in *any* graph the sum of orders of all the vertices is even is called the *handshake lemma*.

(c)   As a consequence of the lemma explain why a graph cannot have an odd number of odd vertices.

(a)   (i) B and C shake hands twice.

      (ii) D shakes hands with herself.

(b) $o(A) = 2$, $o(B) = 4$, $o(C) = 3$, $o(D) = 3$. ($o(A)$ means the order of vertex A.)
      The sum is 12, which is even.

      In general, a handshake involves two people and adds 1 to the order of each of two vertices of the graph. In the exceptional case when someone shakes hands with himself 2 is added to the order of a single vertex. So, starting with the 'null graph' without edges in which the order of every vertex is zero, each handshake (edge) adds 2 to the sum of orders and hence this sum remains even throughout.

      Building up a graph from a null graph in this way and marking in the increases in orders of vertices should make clear the truth of the lemma.

(c)   The sum of an odd number of integers is odd. Hence if the sum of orders is even there cannot be an odd number of odd orders.

Fleury's algorithm

1   Possible answers: the order in which edges are deleted is shown in (a) and (b).

(a)

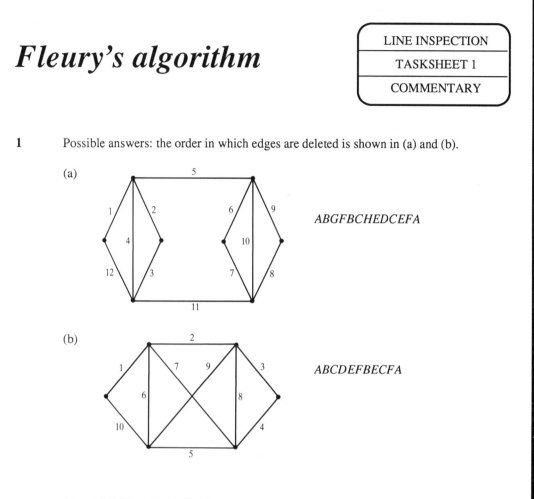

ABGFBCHEDCEFA

(b)

ABCDEFBECFA

(c)   *ABGCDHIFEDFCBFA*

(d)   *ABCDEFABFCEFA*

2   It helps to note at which stages of the deconstruction bridges are left. In particular, in (a), (b) and (c) the edge *AF* is a bridge immediately after the first step *A–B*.

The crux of the explanation is that when a bridge is crossed there is nothing left on one side; for any step *X–Y* which is not across a bridge there is the possibility of later re-entry to vertex *X*. Note that every step in the deconstruction subtracts 2 from the sum of the orders of the vertices.

Planning a sales tour

1 $A - B - C - D - A$
        $60 + 35 + 55 + 90$ $= 240$ miles

2   *BCDAB* is essentially the same tour.

        $C - B - D - A - C$
          $35 + 50 + 90 + 70$ $= 245$ miles

        $D - B - C - A - D$
          $50 + 35 + 70 + 90$ $= 245$ miles

        At this stage the salesman probably thinks 240 miles is the shortest possible distance.

3   If a 'crow's flight' representation is used, *B* lies within the triangle *ACD*.

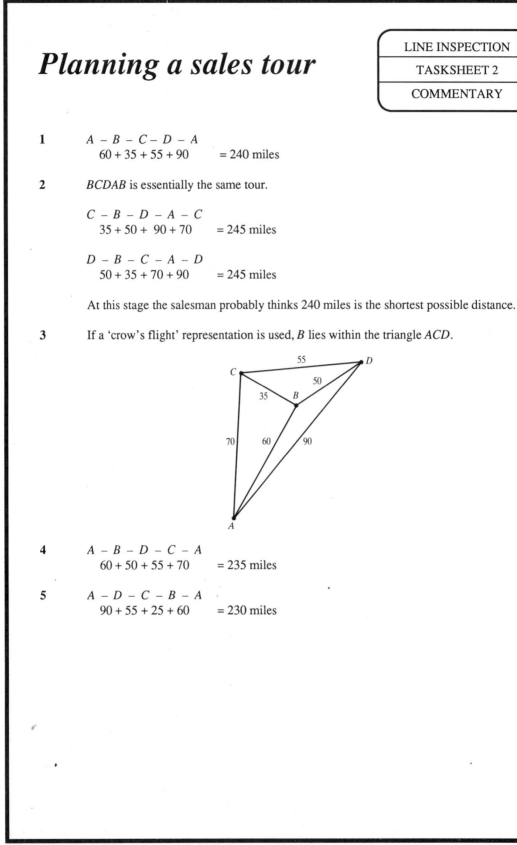

4 $A - B - D - C - A$
          $60 + 50 + 55 + 70$ $= 235$ miles

5 $A - D - C - B - A$
          $90 + 55 + 25 + 60$ $= 230$ miles